# OMG

## That Happened to Me

*——The Cold Bitter Truth——*

# OMG

## That Happened to Me

### —— *The Cold Bitter Truth*——

REA ZINGER

**iUniverse**

# OMG THAT HAPPEN TO ME
## THE COLD BITTER TRUTH

iUniverse books may be ordered through booksellers or by contacting:

iUniverse
1663 Liberty Drive
Bloomington, IN 47403
www.iuniverse.com
1-800-Authors (1-800-288-4677)

ISBN: 978-1-5320-3429-9 (sc)
ISBN: 978-1-5320-3430-5 (e)

Library of Congress Control Number: 2017915304

Print information available on the last page.

iUniverse rev. date: 11/17/2017

# DEDICATION

To my father who died at the age of 47. Too young to be leaving this world so soon. We love you always.

# TABLE OF CONTENTS

# THE COLD DAY

It was a real cold day. My sister and her boyfriend were having a little get together at their house. My boyfriend at the time, him and I went over to their house. After knocking down a few suds, I noticed that it was getting so cold outside. This is not good weather for cars, being a mechanic, I thought that it would be a good idea to let some of the water out of the radiator, to keep the block from cracking.

That night nothing got done, oh well not my car, I could also say not my problem, But I'm the one who would have to fix it when it breaks down.

That night we stayed because we were drinking, and didn't want to any DUIs or DWIs so we stayed, it snowed a little but that is normal for this town. Well the next day I wanted to go home and get some extra stuff, because I wanted to stay a couple days and I didn't have my necessities. That morning was bright, not a cloud in the sky, I even went outside to see how warm it is. It was so warm. So, her and I put summer shorts on and halter tops. We got in the car and headed for my house it was 20 miles away. We were cruising along we got just to the bridge, which is half way, and the car goes POW and the smoke rolls. The car got us another half mile and that's all she wrote. We pulled over to inspect the damage. As we approached the front of the car it starts to snow, and I mean big ass flakes. The temperature drops in a matter of minutes. I'm standing there looking at my sister in amazement what in the hell.!

I felt so stupid, people passing by, looking at these two idiots standing in the middle of a snow storm dressed like that. So, her and I walked to a little store to call my brother to come get us. When he got there, he started laughing at us. We stripped the car and came back for the car the next day. It was the freeze plugs that went out. And that could have been avoided if they would have taken some water out of the radiator. Lesson learned always carry a jacket, or extra clothes with you.

\*\*\*

# PARKING GARAGE

One day it was appointment time for my brother in law. He had to go down town, into a very busy city, I always took him to his appointments. His wife was always working. I didn't mind, him and I get along. On this day, we went down town to see his doctor. You can't park along the street, they will tow your crap away. Been there and did not want to do it again. So, you had to pay an arm and a leg for parking. But we found one, after searching for a half hour. We went into the parking garage and the bottom is full, go figure. To get to the upper levels you had to go up the ramp only made for one car, the sign reads; TURN LIGHTS ON AND BEEP HORN WHILE DRIVING TO NEXT LEVEL; Well big problem there, I have lights but no horn. So while I was driving my brother in law had to stick his head out of the window and holler BEEP, BEEP, BEEP,BEEP,BEEP,BEEP,BEEP. How embarrassing, but if you knew my brother in law and myself, we never cared what people thought. That day after his appointment we had to do the same thing on the way down the parking garage. We got to the gate to leave and nobody would let us out. The gate would not open, finally after a good while, somebody else tried to get out and couldn't, he got someone to open the gate. I don't know if it would be safer to park along the street.

***

# THE BAR

I lived in a rather large city, Its ok. I was living with my parents in the same town. There was this bar right next to where they lived. I went over one day and there was this gut there he was 6'5, tall, dark skin. I played a couple of games with him and went home. Home might have been the wrong word dive, it was not the best of places to live. I went back over to the same bar and he was there. I was so nervous. After a while of knowing him, he asked me to move into this farm house. It had two bedrooms a large kitchen Livingroom, and lots of land to grow whatever, I found that out the first month I was there.

One night he asked me to go out on the town. I thought WOW I have never been out before, this could be a hoot. Well it started when he says put this short skirt on, and this skimpy top, makeup, which I didn't wear. We left for our night out. The first place we stopped was a bar and this bar was, let's just say I was the only person in there that was different. The people were mostly men, drunk. Well coming in here was a bad idea. First thing off the bat the guys started whistling, and making sly remarks about me. The more this went on the more he didn't like it. After about 10 minutes of that he gets so mad that he makes me stand in the corner, until he is done having his fill of beer and cigars. That lasted about three hours. Then it was time to go home, and I couldn't wait. By that time, I was in tears, having to stand there like a dog, I know you thinking why don't she leave. Well it isn't that easy. For one he was two heads taller than me, and I was petrified of him. All this was happening too early in the relationship to be going this shitty already. I'm thinking on the ride home, how can I get out of this nightmare I am in. On the way home, he hits me because I am driving too slow, then he hits me cause I am driving too fast. I got cocky a little and told him; what you can't make up your mind. Well wrong thing, and he stopped the truck and told me to get out. And I did. He drove off and I felt a little relieved. Suddenly here he comes around the corner, stopes the truck and tells me he was sorry, it was the booze talking, it will never happen again. Well dumb me I got back in and went home. That was the start of a wonderful relationship. NOT. You can bet your bottom dollar that they are nice until you got your foot in the door and then bam you're in and can't get out.

Date a good while before jumping into a homestead life. Because they will change like jackal and Hyde. When he puts you out of his truck, stay out ...!!!

***

# THE FARMHOUSE

After meeting this gut in a bar, a while back, we would go look around on Sundays, that seem to be the only day when he wasn't acting like an ass. After a couple of weeks, we found this quant farmhouse. It had lots of yard, fields for planting. That's exactly what he had in mind. He does all the planting and I do all the work. When we moved in it was me, my son and the guy I met and my brother, he was my only brother and he needed somewhere to hang his hat. It was ok, my brother and I got along ok.

That's all, it's nice and quiet. Not for long … After about a month of living ok, it wasn't pleasant all the time but when people weren't around, there wasn't anyone to complicate things. Well one of my sisters and her boyfriend came to visit, but after the weekend they asked if they could stay a couple of days. Now you know I am not going to authorize them to stay there. Of course, he does. Now there are 5 people in the house. Now it seems to be getting a little more tense, around the house, Then another sister decides to come visit and she has baggage. Two kids and a boyfriend. Do you know that they wanted to stay a while, I feel like I'm running a B&B. Now there is 9 people living in our house, and my boyfriend and I were trying to start a family, this situation wasn't working. Maybe it is a sign. My son was a handful at the time, but that's natural this wasn't.

My home only had two bedrooms in it. One was ours and the other was my son's. Little by little things started to change rapidly, he was getting moody, hollering at me more than usual. There were times I would sneak some of his sipping whiskey just to keep from going crazy. Finally, I got pregnant and things just had to change. And they changed from what it was to worse. That winter it got so cold and some of the pipes busted. I am looking around for some strapping man to go under the house and fix the pipes. Nope not a one. If the pipes bust that means that they are not wrapped to keep out the cold. Well under the house I go, I am glad the one of my sisters helped me. She would hold the solder while I heated the pipes, then they had to be wrapped in insolation. Some help they were. After that I thought that would be the end of all things, but nope, life couldn't get any crappier. My other sister wants to come visit, and mom and dad moved in. At one point, there were 13 people in this now small home.

My boyfriend got mad at me for moving all those people moving in. I had to ween, out all but 5 of us. Mom and dad my brother and us. My dad was in the hospital at the time. Things around the house got a little better, not much but some. After it quiet down a little my boyfriend would go down stairs a lot at night. I thought that he had to pee a lot. One night he got up out of bed and I acted like I was sleeping, he would get out of the bed and go downstairs, the bed squeaks really bad, so for me to get out of it so he wouldn't hear me, I would act like I was rolling over in bed, when actually I was getting out of the bed and tiptoe to the end of the railing which overlooks the bathroom door, he would stand at the bathroom door and close it, but he would stand on the outside of it. I guess he would think that he was in there taking one.

Than he would walk to my mother's room which was right under mine and had to listen to them. My stomach would turn. After he was finished going to the bathroom he would come upstairs and stand there to see if I was sleeping. I am 6 months pregnant, I don't know what to do, I am scared to death of him. Later that month dad came home from the hospital. He wasn't well yet. One night we went out for another night of him drinking and making me feel shitty about myself. We came home and walked through the door and into the Livingroom, and there was mom embarking a journey with my boyfriend's much younger son, my boyfriend got very irate and I ended up in the corner with the firewood. I quickly ran outside away from him, and stayed out there all night. I could hear him calling me, say sweet shit nobody wants to hear. Later that night I finally went back in and went up the stairs to our room, which was on the right and my sons room on the left. Not that the story could end here NOPE. He was in my son's room with one of my sisters. Now if that don't break the camel's back. Hurting them did cross my mind. Oh, did it. I turned around went into my room and started tearing everything he bought me, into little dish rags. TIME TO GO.! My advice not that I don't know what I am talking about: don't move family in it is a trap.

## THE END

# THE SODAS

It was like any other day, warm, the sun is out. Well on this day I had to take my brother in law to get some job applications. I had about a half tank of gas. That should be enough to get us to where we had to go. As being the sister in law that was my job driving because he didn't have a driver's license. And filling out the applications, because he was to slow at it, so I got elected.

We must have filled out a hundred applications and it was time to go home before we run out of gas. Well we did. Thank god, we broke down right in front of a gas station. What luck. I didn't have any money on me. He doesn't say anything, so I guess it also my job to go see if I can get any money off the card I had. I went to one place and they couldn't help me, I told him I am going to try another store. I found one but you had to buy ten dollars worth, of stuff before I can get cash back. So I tried that and I managed to get 2 dollars in cash. I go back to the car and my brother in law is drinking a soda, I asked him where in the hell did you get 2 sodas? He said I had a couple of bucks in my pocket and I was thirsty from walking all day, I got you one. Oh I was so irate I started to yell at him. Did you know we were out of gas? He just looks at me with those puppy dog eyes, and if I hadn't been so dam thirsty myself I would have been a whole lot madder. We did make it home. Reminder people when you run out of gas check your brother in laws pockets.

***

# LOCKOUT

It was a cold season. This one year when my son was about a year old I was 19, I was staying with one of my sisters and her boyfriend, he is such a sleaze ball. I never liked the way he treated her, she just let him walk all over her. Him and I have had several runs together. But they asked me to stay with them for a while. Well I did. And it was ok at first but little by little he was getting to demanding, he would stand in front of the icebox when you were trying to get in there.

The electricity you couldn't use, you had to use a flash light to do your bills, and he would bitch about that. They had one of those little apartment washers, that only holds like 2 pair of jeans. It was hard trying to keep the laundry up. He would complain about that. He got a kick out of treating her like shit, I think it made him feel better about himself.

One night my son and I were asleep in the living room, that where we slept while we were staying there. One night I was so tired, I went right to sleep. The next thing I know her husband is standing next to the couch where I was sleeping, I woke up and he was undressed with him man stuff laying on my cheek. GROSS!!. I jumped up and yelled at him, wanted to know what in the hell is he trying to do?. He whispers don't yell you will wake my sister. I couldn't give a rat's ass who I wake up, that's nasty. He actually thought that we were going to have some 3 was ... NOT ...

After that I went to my mom and dads for the evening and to get out of that apartment, come back later. Mom and dad lived a couple of blocks away. We headed there for a while. After the visit, we headed back to my sisters. I am going to have to figure out what to do about what happened last night. I don't know if she knew or not, but that is not happening again. It really starts to put the snow down, so I said my good byes and headed home. I got to the door and knocked on the door, because I didn't have a key, so I knocked and knocked till my knuckles were raw. Then I stood out in the street throwing rocks at the windows, because they lived on the second floor. I could not get anybody to answer the door. I started to drop below freezing, so I headed back to my parent house, thank god, they lived close, or we would of froze to death. After that I asked my parents if I could move back in, I'm not going through that again.

He probably locked me out because I wouldn't put out. I found out just about a year ago that the night that we were standing in the cold knocking on the door trying to get in and throwing rocks at the windows like a dam fool. My sister and he husband were standing a block down the road watching me. Don't ever move in with family no matter how much you love them, and how much you think they love you. That where you find their true colors

## THE END

# THE CARVING KNIFE

I was living in this farm house with my boyfriend and mom and dad, dad being ill at the time, my brother and one of my other sisters, they are everywhere. It was Thanksgiving and at least once a year I like to have a nice meal without the day going to shit. Well NOT …

Dad had made these kitchen knife set for mom a long time ago. Every year we would use them. These things were nice. My dad welded this pitchfork and knife, this was a very big set. Dad didn't fool around when it came to things like that, he was a welder. At one time of his life he was asked to make the railings for these apartments in Georgetown. Because they were filming the exorcist, they needed the railings done, before they could shoot the movie. My father is gone now, died at the age of 47. But I can see his work in the movie.

This set of utensils was his trade, somewhat. On Thanksgiving, my sister and I were preparing the food and she didn't like what I was doing and I told her off and she didn't that. So now we are in a shouting match. She picks up this 2 foot,carving knife and points it at my stomach, which at this point I was 4 months pregnant. I grabbed the fork that goes to the knife. I felt like king Triton, because this thing was so big. I never got cut thank god. We had some more harsh words than made up and went back to what we were doing before the fight. Believe it or not I also still had to go outside and chop and split the wood to keep all these lazy people warm. I had to get these people out of my house. It was too late, in my 5th month I had a miscarriage and lost her. I did get pregnant again, she turned out to be a beautiful woman.

## THE END

# WEST WOODS

B eing a teenager was ok, that's when your fancy free, except the free part, nothing is free. Any way My next youngest sisters were walking home from our girlfriend's home and it's a 5 mile walk but we didn't mind. We walked all the time, to the skating rink. Mainly her and I went the most because we could skate rings around everybody, except pros. Or we would just walk down town and play hide and seek, hiding under the storm drains and grabbing people's legs or just going BOOOOOOO. I know rotten. Well I am sure you were no saint.

We were walking home we got about half way there and this car stopped asked us if we needed a ride. We declined of course. Dad said never hitchhike. There were 2 gentlemen in the car, very homey. Finally, after a couple of no's we said sure got in and we talked to them a little. Than we were home, we said bye but the one dude was very persistent in getting a date with me, I said sure what can it hurt, my dad will have to approve anyway before we can even go out. We set a date and that following Saturday. He had told me he was a ball player, but who knows these days. But he was very muscular so it's possible.

I was a nervous wreck, I couldn't wait till Saturday gets

here. I went to high school the following week not being able to concentrate at all. My hands were shaking. Saturday comes I am about to have a heart attack I'm so nervous. What to wear oh my, what shoes to wear oh my, what draws do I wear oh my, it takes me forever to figure something out, but I do.

I hear this rather loud noise coming from way up the road. It kept getting louder and louder, I went outside to look and up the road comes this nice ass motorcycle. I fell in love. It was him, he took off his helmet and he was handsome of course shaven and smelling like yum. He hands me a helmet I put it on, don't want to crack the old coconut. I got on the bike and then he started it and what a feeling. We took off and rode around for a good while, I felt very comfortable. After a while we were riding through woods, but these woods were starting to get a little thick, a little too thick and then he stops the bike, turns it off. We get off, I asked him what the problem was, or did I need to know. Something started to smell a little fishy. He says that the bike's sparkplug was bad and the bike had to cool down before he could do anything to it. He looks at me like some dumb moron, one you have to get the plug out of the engine before you can tell if it is bad or not. Little does this fool know I have spent about 10 of my years under cars, I was one of those that was under more cars than in them. He was full of it but I just gave him a look of ok. I am more worried about what he had in mind, and it wasn't shop. There was this large oversized tree that had falling down, that I was leaning against. He doesn't walk over put an arm around me maybe neck a little NO, not him, that would just make my day. This fool walks over to me and with more hands then an octopus, more lips than on a 55 gallon, drum, starts manhandling me, when it got to the point of almost complete disaster, I kicked him where the sun don't shine and probably won't for quite some time. I told him to take me home before this becomes a crime scene. He gathers himself gets on the bike and starts it and what a surprise it started. He took me home and I never told me father about that because there would have been even bigger trouble for him. I didn't see him for a couple of weeks I can understand, time to heal the jewels. One day in cooking class I had a friend who was telling me about her guy stuff, juicy gossip. She started telling me about this guy tall muscular, blond hair, and the motorcycle ha had, I almost lost it. Than she was tell me about this bitch that was mean to him, she even explained what furniture was in her house. I couldn't do anything but look at her with my mouth open. What? I told her about my last boyfriend or still boyfriend I don't know. But I am for sure now. I told her that guy was my boyfriend, I didn't know what to expect. Slap in the face, crying, hysteria. No she says let's get him good. I was blown away. We found out where he was playing ball and decided to pay him a visit at the field. Her and I stood there right at home plate, so when he came in for a run he would run alright, right into us. He's coming in home plate, he scores and stands up brushes himself off and looks up and sees us together, puts his head down and walks off. GO HOME TEAM

## THE END

# THE MISSING FURNITURE

I lived in a one room shack with my first husband and my son and my daughter. This place was for the rats, bums outside, people making noise all hours of the night. On top of that we lived right along a busy highway. It was a three ring, circus. One day I was with my girlfriend, she was making a phone call at the pay phone in front of the building. As she was talking to her girlfriend and she was going on about this guy that was making passes at her and asking her for a date, my girlfriend's brother, him and my husband hung out together and he happen to know the chic, Her, brother confirmed it. I waited for my hubby to come from work and get him good. I talked to the girl, I wasn't mad at her just the situation. I got her name for later. Hubby comes in it is dinner time. I have one extra place for dinner, he, ask, why? Oh, I met the girl and she is going to come over for dinner. He asked who? I said her name. and he starts stuttering like an idiot. What's the matter dear, you alright? She really wasn't really coming, but what a got you moment.

Our marriage went to hell. He wouldn't hold a job, he would steal from his job and get fired because of it, and too stupid to return it to get his job back. It just could not work. I had enough, we even went to church to help us work through this. And I gave him another try, we were doing ok, moving at a good pace in our life and one day I was washing dishes in a sink so small it takes you forever to do one plate. I'm agitated that everything is difficult. I had to be the bread winner and he is the man, he was laying on the couch in the middle of the day I'm cleaning, what wrong with this picture. I was almost finished with the dishes, him and I got into it, due to being useless. He calls me a slut, I stopped what I was doing, went over to the couch where his ass sat all day, and the day before. I yanked off the couch, I mashed him, He wanted to be a couch potato. Live it. Afterwards he lay back down on the couch bleed all over everything, fueling the fire, and you believe he still, after all that he started running his chops again, and I walked over to him and informed him of his rights and that he didn't have any. I went back to what I was doing. The next day we were talking about splitting up and who gets what. The only thing in the apartment that was a sofa, love seat, 5, inch, black and white tv, and the cloths on our backs. One day when he wasn't there I talked to our maintenance guy and he agreed to put all the stuff in the apartment into storage and tell him that I talked to a lawyer and he said to sell all of our stuff and split the cash. So that's what I did. When he got home it was all gone. I handed him 50 cents and he says what's this? A lawyer said to sell everything and give you half. Here you go. He got so mad, had a fit. He stormed out. I had the maintenance guy put it back into my apartment. I went to work the next day and I got home and everything was gone, and so was he. Lesson learned, when they leave change the locks.

***

# THE DUMPSTER

I lived in a small town, you could throw rock from end to end. I lived in a small home, with my son, boyfriend, and my mother. My boyfriend would always come from work and mom always trying to put her two cents in. She would always holler at him for getting something to eat. The first thing out of her mouth is, why is your ass always hanging out of the refrigerator? But instead of him saying something to her, he would complain to me in bed about how nasty she is to him. Well dear if you don't want her to talk to you like that, then say something to her. I fought enough with her when I was growing up. The next day he came home and opened the refrigerator door and she started. Get out, he turned around and told her to shut the hell up and to mind you own dam business.

After that we started to get along and it was our monthly trip to the dump, because we had to dump our own trash, and sometimes we would find some cool stuff. My motto is someone else's trash is to someone else's treasure. Before you could go through the dumpsters and find some good stuff, strollers, baby beds, plastic flowers, picture frames, etc ... but now they don't want you to do that anymore due to safety reasons. So that night we went to the dump to dump our trash and look around. It was dark enough to not get into any trouble, if a car came we just act like we are dumping. My boyfriend jumped into this one dumpster to get something out of it and mom and I were at another one, there was about 25 dumpsters, we see the truck coming, hopefully he is just passing by. Nope he turns into the road and backs his truck right up to the one my boyfriend is in, out of all the ones here. My mom and I ran, she went to the left and I went to the right to get behind the dumpster and we ran right into each other knocking us both down, and causing me to need a diaper at that point of time. We couldn't stop laughing, rubbing our foreheads, now that I think about it when we are in mischief moms there. Now my boyfriend is still trapped in this thing, the guy with the truck grabs a handful of stuff to throw into the dumpster, my boyfriend pops up from where he was and that poor man screamed dropped his stuff got in his truck and hauled ass.

We laughed so hard, I hope he was ok after that. We went back to what we were doing, now someone else is coming it is a cop, I thought that old man ratted on us, we quickly act like we are dumping as usual, the cop pulls up to us and says, it works better if you use a flashlight. We stood there, said thanks and he rolled out. What a night. It goes to show you, there is treasure where ever you look, you just got to know where to look.

***

# DC MUSIC CLUB

Wow new school, new people I don't know. I didn't like it at all, I was alone in this white world. I did, I met this girl and we hit it off, we would hang out at her house, which was about 2 blocks away from the school. She had it made, wait till the entire school leaves then walk home. Us me and my older sister and my next youngest sister, we had to ride the bus home, I really didn't mind so much about the name calling but I draw the line of physical contact. Well isn't it ironic how when everything is going so good turn to crap so fast. It was the end of the year and it was SAT time, well during lunch my girlfriend and I were having lunch and this dark chick comes over to me and takes my cake right off my plate, I didn't care about that cake, she can have it, no this stupid bitch I call a friend goes to the principal that was leaning against the stage and tells him, why? I don't know, she just got me into a bunch of trouble with these girls. I was so mad, she can wait to go home I had to ride the bus with them. After lunch, I went up to the girl and told her that I didn't tell him about the cake, but all I did was make it worse I think, the rest of the day went ok, I dodged a bullet. At the end of the school they call certain buses and we go to the auditorium and then the buses. I want out of here. We lined up at the door and from behind someone pinched me so hard I saw stars. I pushed so hard to get out of this building and I,hit the door, and I ran for it, and all of a sudden I was hit from behind, I hit the ground hard. I get up as fast as I could, my bus was still yards away, I get up and run for the bus and again I am hit from behind. This time I did know what hit me, it was a tuba case and the tube still in it because I heard it ring when it hit me both times, I'm dazed, no idea where to go now, I can't see anything with blurred vision, got to get up. I managed to get to my feet and weave through a couple of buses to get rid of them. Nope. They hit me again and I hit the ground hard, got to get to the bus, got up got to the bus she opened the door and now they are kicking me, I don't even get a foot on one of the platforms before their, on me. They kicked me in the head, ribs, back, the face. It lasted what seemed like hours, they gave me a break, I crawled onto the steps of the bus and sat in the seat closest to the bus driver, wondering why she isn't helping me, she just sat there. to my surprise my 2 sisters were already on the bus, I asked where were you when they were kicking the shit out of me? We didn't know it was you. And we didn't want to get into it. I can understand that, I wouldn't, being scared. The bus got us home and I had to go to the hospital, broken ribs, bad concussion, and look like I was attacked by a dog. My dad got the people involved. We had found out that the same group of kids paralyzed the bus driver. The next year school was going to be a real hoot, if it anything like last year, I'm out. The year started out ok, no problem with the bad kids. Well one day

I was in gym class and wasn't participating, I just wanted to be by myself. I go to the almost top of the bleachers and sit there doing some work I had to do, these 2 girls come into class and they climb the bleachers right where I happen to be sitting. They sit behind me, I don't like that, so I moved and they follow, of course. They were eating in class which is not permitted. They got up and dumped the box of pretzel salt in my hair. What do I do? If I tell I'm in trouble, if I don't than they win. It is only my life, maybe I can live with crunchy hair. I got up and walked down there told the teacher and she sent them to the office. I heard a later bitch and the other one pushed me, I am going to pay for that later. I waited a couple of days and nothing, great. Spoke too soon. All a sudden from behind something hits me hard and slams me into a concrete wall, I fall, books go flying. Dam it, this shit had to stop. I got up and as I stood I had my back to her, I rolled my fist turned around as fast as I could and punched her right in the neck and she hit the ground, I didn't want to do that I wanted to sock her in the face, and she flinched back to keep me from hitting and I caught her in the neck, my blood was boiling, I could of ripped the head something, that how much adrenaline was in me, the bad kids that are usually picking on me are actually cheering me on, I felt empowered. Oh back to the girl, now she in on the ground turning blue, I must have somehow when she flinched, I hit her, she swallowed her tongue, that's the only thing I can think of. I picked up on of those heavy ass science books and smacked her in the back of head as hard as I could to keep her from chocking, Of course.

After that school was ok, we finally got to move to a better place. Dad taught that if you get your ass beat don't come crying, you beat their asses. Words spoken of a true father.

## THE END

# THE CAR BED

One weekend my son and I went to see my mom and his grandmother. The visit was ok I guess. The woman had a very busy life style. She had men coming in at all hours of the night. That weekend I met this guy and he seem ok, a little of the beaten path, but ok. He asked me and my son if we wanted to go do his place in the mountains, a little forward but I said yes and my son was all for it, so we went with him in his car and we drove a while, wow this house is way back in the woods. You could get lost. My son found it great, he gets out of the car and starts to play, so that's a good sign. Meanwhile him and I went into the house, now this house had no curtains, no carpet, no stove, there was a wood stove, hardly no furniture. That wasn't anything bad, I had less as a child, this place needed a woman's touch. The floor was wood slats, you could almost see dirt. Outside was woods and more wood, the yard needed a bush hog and mow down some those big weeds. The whole place was rugged but livable. While we were there he asked me and my son if we wanted to move in, I barely knew him. He said what a better way to get to know one another, I agreed. The place I was in was expensive, I guess now I can give the rats, cockroaches, and the mice back their home. I packed all our stuff up, and took all the money we had on a U-Haul.

I think my son was more excited to move than I was, but the city was no place for a young boy. We are on our way. After about 3 hours of driving we pull up at mom's, the man that I was going to move in with was already at my mom's house, why doesn't that surprise me. I got out of the truck and he walks over to me, gives me a kiss on the cheek, like a gentleman. I said are you ready to go I'm all packed. He says I can't let you move in with me. I am standing there in amazement, what just happened, I was only gone for a few days, did I go through some time warp. I went upstairs and asked my mother what was going on with him? He said that we are not moving in with him. I'm thinking to myself that bitch, she had something to do worth him changing his mind. She says oh I'm so sorry to hear that in a sarcastic way, I know she was involved. What am I going to do? I have a truck full of our lives and nowhere to put it, no money, I spent it all on the truck.

I asked mom if I could stay with her for a couple of months, just until I start getting my stuff transferred up here, she said no. My other 2 sisters stay there with their boyfriends rent free. And I'm offering to pay you. Still no. I left moms and walked down to the little town to think, I couldn't drive the truck, had to save the gas. We walked down town and walked a while so I could think, my son's legs were getting tired so we sat in front of a little store. I didn't even have any money to get my son a hot cocoa. What am I going to do? I sat in front of this store I put my hands over my face and Syed. My son says to me, mommy why don't grandma love us? Where are we going to sleep? I told him that grandma needs help and start acting like a grandma and as far as the sleeping arrangements I will have to figure that one out.

I grabbed my son by the hand and said we are going back to grandmas and make her see it my way, but mommy she doesn't love us, I know. We went back there and I had to give up all my check for rent and all my food stamps. For about 6 months my son slept on the couch, and I was the only paying mom for rent. My sisters got a room to their selves, not fair at all, but I didn't want to make waves. She would have parties all night long, people coming in drinking, falling down, punching holes in the walls, fighting. My son had to get up for school, and having to deal with that all night. Me myself I slept in the back of my sister's boyfriend's car. I did that for 6 months. Finely one month I didn't pay mom and said that they mixed something up at SS, and I would pay her next month extra, I needed to do that so I would have enough money for the security deposit, and the next month you can bet we were out of there. This place was a whole lot better. I feel bad on the way I had to deceive her but she left me no choice.

I guess I underestimated the love she had, apparently it was none.

## THE END

# MAN EATING DUMPSTER

On a warm summer, I was living in the back of a bar, strange but it works. There were several apartments there. That morning I wake up to the smell of burnt bacon, I open my eyes and my son had a full breakfast on a tray, the bacon was a little black, the eggs were brown, the toast was burnt, but I didn't care, he made it with his own two hands. It was so sweet. I ate everything. That evening my sister and her boyfriend, which I don't really care for, they came to visit, their son was the same age as mine and when it came time for them to go home my son wanted to go too, I couldn't say no, but I had no way to come up and get him, by brother in law said I will bring him home. That's 188 miles and I don't have a car. He left with them for a couple of weeks, I am going to worry the whole time he is up there. A couple of weeks go by and they haven't brought him home yet. I called and he said he wasn't bringing him home, I knew this was going to happen. I had to get the money to get someone to take me up there and get my boy.

I got up there and he gave me some story of why he couldn't bring him, since he said he would. I got there and talked to my sister for a while my son gathers his stuff. I went to tell my son something and my brother in law said that I couldn't talk to him while he is staying there, well he isn't staying because I am leaving soon and with my boy, well you can't talk to him, as long as he is in my home. I don't give a rat's ass where he is, I'm going to talk to him whenever I want and if you don't like that well oh well. Him and I got into it and I just stopped, he is not worth it, he stormed off and grabbed some trash bags and headed for the trash dump. My sister asked me if I was going to let him talk to me that way I said no. God will take care of him, if he thinks he is going to talk to me like he talks to her, not. I talked to her for a while and started to leave, when he came back from the dumpsters. He was holding a towel to his head. My sister asked him what happened and he said that he fell in the dumpster and cut his ear, really bad, enough to need stiches. I thought that was one of the funniest things that I ever had the pleasure of not having to do it myself. I gathered my son and his things and got the hell out of there. Just remember. GOD SEES ALL.

\*\*\*

# MONSTER ANT

My older sister and I always noticed this old house on our way back home from school, it looked inviting, come rob me, one day on the way when nobody was looking we cut into the bushes and wait for everybody to away. When the coast was clear we went up to the old house, it didn't look like anyone was living in it. We tried to get inside but it was closed tighter than a drum. DAM. I really wanted to get inside and find stuff. That was not going to happen. But there was a bunch of boxes on the front porch filled with all kinds of goodies. We found one box full of ties, we used them to tie together to make a swing out of, and the rest we kept for father's day, and his birthday, what? We were poor.

After we tied all the ties together we walked over to this peach tree to tie us up a swing. The peaches were in bloom. Just as we got over to the tree, we noticed something in the tree, it was an ant, I'm not talking an ant you can squish with your fingers. We stood there for the longest time, scared to move. This thing was the size of a dog, its head was the size of a melon, its legs were like foldup chair legs, its tentacles were like the ones you have on your house.

It was very big, it was eating a rotten peach. We went home and told nobody because if we did nobody would believe us and then we would have to explain why we were there. I'm thinking alien ant.

\*\*\*

# THE HEADLESS HORSEMAN

The hell house is what I called it. Paranormal sure, creepy you bet, this was where the system put us when things didn't go right. Foster care. It was ok at first because we were getting something to eat,once in a while. Time goes by and now I'm being moved to another home, why I do not know. But you do what they say, and off to another foster home. Got there and it was where my older sister and my next youngest sister were, happy, happy. Too good to be true, turn my frown upside down. No hey, hello it was hit the fields, what are we going to do, I just got here? You came just in time, why? Now we get to chop the tobacco down than we would have to spear it and then it gets hung in the barn, 5 hours of back breaking work, I was waiting for the cold glass of lemonade, water? No we aren't done working. Now we have to mow about a thousand archers it was all you could see was land, thank god, we only had to mow half of it. After that we had to go fight with 2 horses so we can get the manure out of their pen, they didn't like us there, then we had to go take the now smelly shit and hoe in the garden for about an hour, my god it was my first day and I'm half dead. Now we are done. We scrubbed our feet with lye soap that was made last week. By this time, it was dark, I am hungry, no food, doesn't she feed you all? Yes, but not this late. Now we go to bed. I was so tired I hadn't noticed how cold it was upstairs. After a while it was visitation with our parents. The place called and they are only going to take 2 of us to visit, it was hard, I lost and didn't get to go. That really sucked because I will have to do all the work around here myself. After they left for their visit I went to work I wanted to get all of my work done before it got dark, because it is creepy around here after dark. So I wanted to get it done now. Finally done and hell with eating I'm too tired. I go to sleep rather quickly and what seemed like minutes, i woke up and I was floating in space, no bed, no window, no nothing, just stars and lots of them, I couldn't even feel the bed I was laying on. I closed my eyes and kept saying wake up, your dreaming, I open my eyes and the room was where it was when I went to sleep. That next day was inside clean day all beds linens, floors the entire kitchen. The morning of them to come home, the old lady is screaming at me, she is in my older sister's room and the end of the covers were pulled back like someone is going to bed, but she pulled the covers back and there as a streak of blood from the middle of the pillow all the way down to to the feet. I didn't leave it like that and i haven't started my cycle then, and getting yelled at for the attic doo always open. You close it, and it would be open the next morning.

It is time for them to come back, and I can't wait. When they got back it was back to the grind, On the weekends she let up have some fun time, if that means playing in the soy beans, or go see if we can get the horses to chase us. The only thing about that her nieces and nephews would drop by and treat us like a bunch of peasants, they would ask us to play with them but they would make us the bad people or someone they can order you around in fun and get a kick out of it. Once one of her nieces wanted to play I dream of genie and of course she wanted me to be the bad genie, well I didn't want to disappoint her, so I crossed my arms and blinked and put her into a pretend jar and the went to play with my sisters and left her there, I'm sure she went crying to granny, but nothing happened. On Saturday's we had to do the inside of the house before we could play, but that was nothing compared to outside work. But during the cleaning she would carry this tray of coffee or tea cookies or cut sandwiches into this room which was right across from my next youngest sister and me. She would unlock it walk in and close the door behind her, be in there for about 10 minutes and come out with an empty tray. We would really try to sneak a peek when she wasn't looking. We asked her what was in there and she said, you stay away from that room, nobody go in there, this lady was about 80 years old with a German accent.

We let that go for now. We will investigate. I was tired and wanted to go to bed, but it was cold in there, she always kept a big rag in the register to keep the heat downstairs. I pulled it out one night and she was sitting on the couch sleeping with her head back and her mouth open and when I moved the rag, a big wad of dust went right in her mouth, I couldn't have done that again. She yelled at us to put that back in there. I just wanted some heat stingy bitch.

We would always wait till she went to bed and waited until we knew she was out of it and we would sneak into the pantry where she kept the canned stuff nothing worth getting into. BUT, she did have a good supply of dog food, good enough for them. She bought 50 pounds of gravy train and 50 of the chuck wagon. She opened the gravy train first. We would open a napkin and fill then with gravy train, and sneak back upstairs and sit in bed crunching on dog food. This was ok, and it doesn't taste any better with water, you know for the gravy, it nasty, looks good but it isn't. We needed a change of pace so I had to figure out how to get into the chuck wagon bag without her finding out. Maybe there is and she will know about it. You see I took a fork and scratched the bottom of the bag so it will look like mice did it, and it worked, she was hot but blamed it on the mice, we told her we would put some traps down. Never did. That was worth almost getting caught. It tasted a lot better than the gravy train.

One day she left to go to the store. Now we have a chance to get into that room and see what is going on. We picked the lock and we were in. God, we were so nosy. The room was big and warm not like ours, the bed was overstuffed with big feather blankets, pillows, not like our bedroom cold blankets look like they were in the civil war the pillow looked like chicklets flat as a pancake, this was not fair at all why can't we sleep in this room? We opened the closet and in there were these gowns like from the 1800s. These were priceless. The one I had tried on was pine green and had a square neckline, with emblements all over it. Under the dress was this plastic skirt that made the dress really wide, it had puffed sleeves, silky material. My older sister had on one that was maroon with gold trim on it, the material was thick like curtain material. It was real thick, my other sister, the one she had on was yellow, and somewhat like the one I was wearing. We felt like Cinderella. We scrubbed floors like her and didn't get to go to the ball. These dresses felt wonderful. All a sudden we hear a car coming, we look out the upstairs window it was her we got to get out of this room. We took the dresses off as fast as we could without ripping them, put them back in the closet and got the hell out of there, locked it the same way unlocked it. She never found out that we were in there.

Winter is here, and we were in bed freezing to death, every

time we try to pull that rag out of the vent she yells at us. One cold ass night, the wind was howling, more than usual. We were listening to our little am-fm radios that mom and dad gave us, nut we had to hide them because she would take them from us. One night we were listening to the music and we thought we heard a bang noise we turned to music off and listened, nothing, we went back to the radios and we heard another noise, it sounded like a horse riding up the road, like when they are on pavement, but there was nothing but dirt out there, so maybe we were hearing things, a few more minutes go by and we hear a loud bang, this should of woke up half the neighborhood. But nothing. We were afraid to move, the bang made the house shake, then metal noises, then the window opened, and the snow was just rolling in. Out covers were so holey there wasn't much to cover with. The moon was shining so bright that it was beaming right into the bedroom. The next thing something was coming in the window oh no what do we do? Nothing, lay there and don't move. Whoever or whatever was in our room went over to the dresser where we had all, of our powders, hairbrush, nail polish, you know all those girlie things and swooped them all on the floor, you could hear stuff rolling across the floor, the it went over to this cabinet we used as a closet and ripped everything out on to the floor, I am shaking and about to run out of that room, but if we did we would have to run right past him. That is not going to work than it came over to the bed, I had to try to see what it was, I couldn't stop shaking, we peeked through the holes in the covers to see something. It came over and it started to run its hands across the covers, we could feel him searching the bed looking for something, the only thing I saw was something human shaped but had no head just shoulders. He picked something up off the bed which there wasn't anything there and put it under his arm and it leaped out of the window and was gone. We didn't even get up to see the damage the it did. The next morning the old lady came upstairs and was screaming at us for making this mess, but we didn't do it. There was about 3 foot,of snow on the floor, the floor is covered in powder and a lot of broken things, the cloths were all out of the closet on the floor. She said that there was a ladder leaned against the house and she tell us that we were trying to escape. I told her if we were going to escape we would have had to jump of the roof and get a ladder and climb back in, if we were going to escape we would have had to jump off the roof and kept on going. We cleaned all the mess up and kept that dam window locked.

## THE END

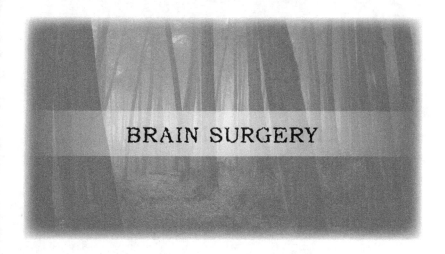

# BRAIN SURGERY

eing young tends to get you into some trouble, so instead of trouble we me and some of my other sisters, thought that since by baby sister is such a pain in the rear, she would follow you around and be annoying. We told her that we wanted to give her brain surgery and put another one in a better and new and improved brain. She said ok, that's the spirit. We made a ER under the peach tree. We used dad's tools, mom's kitchen utensils, some sheets, we had to make it look real, she was gullible. We are ready for the patient, we took blue napkins and rolled them in dirt, those are going to be the ones we show her when she wakes up, and some clean yellow ones to show her what we are putting in her when she is in surgery. We give her a smarty candy, told her that it was a sleeping pill and she should be asleep soon. Believe it, she went to sleep and slept for about an hour. When she was out we took marker and drew stitches on her forehead and when she woke up we told her what we did and what we took out of her. She was so different after that, not as annoying. I guess it was the placebo effect.

\*\*\*

# THE CAMPING TRIP

My older sister and her husband, they finally married. My husband, I was married at the time. We all decided to get out from under the everyday stuff. We decide to go camping in another city away from it all. Planning it was a pain, but we figured it all out. Well this seems to be going ok, and just before we leave we had to take this kid with us, I was babysitting him for his mom while she was at work. This was our time, dam it. Because we would not be back till the beginning of the week we just took him with us. I loved him, but not enough to drag him along, I had drinking planned, you know falling down, and we also had some real good smoke for later. We got to our destination and my brother in law didn't want to pay the extra few dollars to stay there, so we headed further out of town, even out of state and stopped at this little store and did our whatever we had to do. We headed to this other place and it started to hail, I don't mean little ice balls, these things were huge. While the guys are in the office this boy is yanking on my shirt, what do you want? I had to go poo, we were just at the gas station why didn't you go then? Of course, I didn't have to go then. So now my brother in law wants to go back where we were before to camp, I wish people would make up their minds on what it is that they are doing. We are back where we were. And we started unpacking the car, thank god it wasn't hailing here, it was warm and sunny. We try to set up the tents and it starts to thunder and lightning, the boy did not like that one bit, the whole time we were trying to put up the tents he was standing there with a boogie board from out of the back of the car, and has it over his head screaming the lightning was going to get him, what a pain. Finally, we got them up and because it started to rain and I mean like Noah's ark was coming through we put the doors to the tents together. That day was shot to hell, and now I can't drink because when I drink I pee a lot and the bathrooms are somewhat close, but I could go outside but we had boogie boy with us. My shoes were outside the tent soaked I'm sure. My brother in law lite the lanterns we had, but he put fuel in them instead of kerosene and when he lite them they started shooting flames out of it, it almost caught the food on fire. We gave up trying to get anything done, so we put everything in the cars and went to sleep or just lay down. The next day everything was soaked. We wanted to have some coffee first and then get into the beer and sipper later. Not so easy, well in haste of putting everything away we managed to lock both sets of keys in my sister's purse and the purse was in the car locked up. What next? We did happen to have a hammer we were using it for the tents. We got the window open and got the keys and had our coffee and decided to take our loses and cash out, see if they would give us some of our money back, and they did. We headed home. As the trip progressed we would write messaged on them and drive along their car so they could read them and back and forth, we did this till we were home, that made the trip a whole lot quicker. When we got home we finished what we started. My brother in law and I were playing spin the bottle and bogie boy wanted to play. I told him that he could not play because you had to go by the rules and I know he could not do them. I said ok and I spun the bottle and it landed on bogie boy and I said truth or dare? He says dare. Ok I told him that he would have to sit in that chair and not move for 5 minutes. He sat there for the 5 minutes, I didn't think he had it in him. Well it was his turn to spin the bottle and it lands on me I take a dare. In my back yard, I have the shed with crap in it. He wanted me to run up to the building and that hit the ground like they do in the westerns. I said ok, a little odd but ok. I started at one end of my yard and ran towards the shed, and when I got to it, I was supposed to hit the ground. No, I run, I get to the shed and went right through them. I hit a pile of smashed cans and then the rake came down and cracked me in the head then the shovel, then the rest of the can that were stacked in there. Everybody outside all they heard was things falling on me. My feet were the only things sticking out of the shed. We ended up making the best out of a bad situation.

## THE END

# POKER MOM

I was a teenager, barely. I did a lot when I had no responsibilities, party, stay out late and hope that your dad isn't going to catch you. The drive in those were the day, I sounded old but I had to start work, I had to support a beautiful boy, he was almost 2, and I worked just a couple of blocks from my home. My mother was watching my son for me, while I worked. While I was working, after work my mom would walk my son half way to see me top the hill from work, he would always pick me some kind of flower for me, even though they were always too short to put into water.

One day I was coming home from work and so son, no flower, no mom, what's going on. This worried me. I was thinking all kinds of things. When I got home I could not see anyone, as I went down the hall there was the person that is supposed to be watching my son, was playing strip poker with the guy I dated. I am wondering where in the hell my son is while she is trying to work her way through the yellow pages. I was very unhappy to say the least. Later I found out that his own mother, a church lady found out and grounded him for life. I never let her watch my child again, That, goes to show you never leave your important things that are close to you with people that are bound to self-destruct.

***

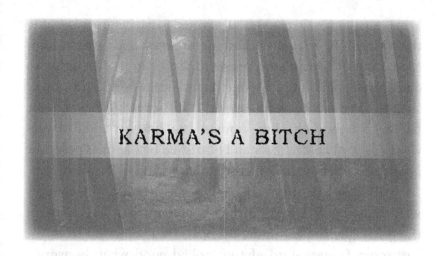

# KARMA'S A BITCH

aving a lot of siblings, it is hard to get along with them, one of my sisters I had big issues she was always daddy little girl it seemed. My older sister had the same problem with her. That was ok with me, that way I would have someone on my side, and we can pick on her together. One day, dad come home and said that his sister gave him tickets to a classical concert. I thought that they were just for him and mom, but he said that we could go. Mom and dad and my older sister and me, and her, why does she have to come? I wouldn't dare say that out loud, dad would have handed my one in the chops. He was strict but attentive, he drank but I would too if I had to live her, oh I do.

We get to the concert and this place was breath taking, the ceilings were decorated and the grand staircase running down both sides of the hall. I died and went to heaven. I didn't care about anyone else because I am the only one that would listen to classical music with my father, right after work, I would put his records, sometimes so many the turntable would drag from the weight of the records.

Was this worth sitting hours with hot curlers in your hair.

Yes' it was, so far. Of course,dad wanted to eat before we went to the concert. We go to this Chinese restaurant and ordered chow Mein, and of course miss priss didn't like it, it taste nasty, so dad got her something else and that made me boil, daddy's little suck up. We saw the concert and it was great. Well everyone had to go to the bathroom. Woman went one way and dad went where ever. My older sister and I finished before miss priss, she is probably looking in a mirror and cracking it, I'm sure.

The lobby was pretty, the lights, the people and what they were wearing. We had gowns on but nothing like some of the other guest, I felt under dressed. Dad shows up from the bathroom I guess. Dad always looked good when he wore a suit, it wasn't often but when he did, he looked good. Mom, dad and my older sister were still waiting on the queen to make her big entrance, so she can impress dad. Well here she come miss America, she waits at the top of the stairs, swooshes her hair back, as to set her pose for stardom. We are just about to hurl, come on. She starts down the steps get about to the third step and she trips and topples to the bottom of the stairs, I thought that I was going to dye laughing, my sister next to me was laughing too. Dad gave her and I one of those death looks, like shut up or I will come over there. It did not work, we laughed even harder, she finally got hers. I love it when it works in our favor. We laughed all the way home, even after. It works, just when someone you think should get their just reward, god will prevail.

\*\*\*

# OVER PROTECTIVE DAD

One morning I had to go to school, and I didn't want to. Mom would make you. One day I had my shoes and she made me wear my brother's shoes, they were 2 sizes too small for me, she would make me wear them anyway. One night I got sick and I didn't feel good the next morning. I told mom I didn't want to take lunch, I was still not feeling good. You think mom would let me stay home, but no. I go to school and it was lunch time and we all lined up by the door with lunch in hand except mine because I didn't bring one. The adult in the room, got really mad at me for no reason. I did not have my lunch with me. I did not know that it was a crime not to have your, lunch. This person used rulers for child correction and it hurt very much. All I could do was to cry and scream. I sat down at my desk, I was 8 then. My hand started to swell, I cried and the teacher kept telling me to stop that whimpering. I held back as much as I could I didn't want to set her off. I went home and mom didn't say much, she iced my hand and said we will see what your father says. I know what he going to do, no doubt in my mind.

Dad get home and I let him settle in before I spring this

on him, but I couldn't wait my hand hurt bad and I went in the living room and told him what had happened, and at first, he was calm, he rewrapped my hand in ice and gave me that everything is going to be alright speech, it helped. The next morning dad was on fire and was up early, he grabs his sawed off, shot gun and went to the school, he wouldn't have hurt anyone unless they got in his way. We got to the school walked in or should I say he walked and I was being dragged by the hand, the good hand. He walked right to the principal's office and right into his office, right passed the secretary, dad started to yell at this man and this man had no ideas what he was talking about. Dad yanked me across the desk and showed him my fist which was about the size of an orange. Dad asked him if he was in the practice of beating children at school, what kind of school are you running here? What happen sir. One of your staff did this to my daughter. I did not want to tell my Father about what took place earlier before the ruler beating. I finally told, both, of them, what happened before. The staff member asked us to staple our papers together and to get in line. I did so. Right when it was my turn to staple my paper, I placed the paper in the stapler and got ready to staple my paper, she said everyone sit down. I finished pushing the stapler down. It was about 3 seconds. She grabbed me by the are and stood me in front of the class, lifted me dress and smacked me with about two rulers. It still hurt. When I said that it made dad even more mad. The Principal said that he would take care of it and that there wouldn't be any more problems. Dad said good. If there is any other problems I will be back and I will have my friend with me. Pointing the gun in the air as to be talking about it. The next day I came to school and was told to go to the guidance office. I did, and they gave me a class number to go to. I got there and there was a teacher sitting there with a smile on her face.

She waved me towards her. I was hesitant but did. She asked me if I was ok. I said yes. I told her that my hand hurt and that I had a headache. She gave me an aspirin and a sip of her soda she had on her desk. I sat where she told me to sit. The rest of the day was great. Later that week she took me to get some cloths and stuff. Mom and dad were ok with that. Whoever you are thank you for your help.

## THE END

# THE SOUTHERN STRANGER

I was young and dropped out of school, I'm going to run away with this guy I met, we dated a couple of times, he was 18 years older than me, I guess he was the charmer. But I figure if I don't leave, my mother might get her claws into him, I really didn't get a chance to get into know him. We left that morning. We ended up in another town and then we were going somewhere else.

We left the next morning from where ever I was and we filled up, and we were on the road. 18 hours later we were across some states, this one was hot. We pulled up to someone's bungalow, or shanty, it was small and square. I stepped out of the car and stepped right into an ant hill. They bit me all over my feet, what a home coming. They stung like bees. I went inside and wanted some water, I was dry from that long drive, I started to get water out of the tap and the guy there stopped me and said you can't drink the water here to salty. You got to boil it several times just to drink it. We lived there for a little while.

Everyone wanted to go to the beach, so we grabbed a cooler and filled it with beer, liquor, ice. Off to the beach we go. It was breath taking, and hot as hell, 108' degree in the shade. Him and I wanted to walk out to the light house, this light house was out in the water, surrounded with water and the only way to get to it is on these square rocks, the further you go out the bigger the gaps get. One time he was talking to me and I disappeared between the rocks. Once he pulled me up we headed back to the beach. The rock wall ran all the way onto the beach and on.

Later he wanted to go get something at the little dinner that was at the end of the dyke. They made a burger that cost 6 dollars and its worth every penny. Well he left and I was there fishing by myself, getting ripped out of my mind. He never came back so I sat up all night fishing and drinking, I don't have a clue where in the hell he is. I keep fishing and I get a bite, and its giving me a fit, I finally pull it up on shore. I thought that maybe I had too many drinks but it looked like a hand, I hesitated a while and when I get the nerve to go over there, the fingers started moving, I leaped back. There is no body attached to it so it should not be moving, but it is. I got the balls to go over there and I touched it and it was a plat-tex glove filled with minnows. Well at least I had a hand on things.

I fell asleep on the beach, and woke up with one hell of a hangover, he said I got you one of those sandwiches you like up there at the dyke. I went up to the truck and on the seat, was something that used to look like my sandwich. This sandwich had a perfect butt print in the middle of it, you're thinking how is that possible, well the burger is about 6 inches in diameter. Now it's a 12 inches round. I asked him what in the flying Dutchman is this? Where were you? No answer. But I do know what he did and what he did it with. I went back to the beach and noticed I was out of Alcohol. All day he would be out in the water, and holler I'm drowning, I run out there, swim to save him and he laughs at me. After doing that a couple of times and ruin a watch and a very nice lighter, I left dum dum at the beach, and I went to the small tavern there to get a beer. I ordered a beer, picked it up and dropped it upside down on the floor, I ordered another one and did it again, the third time this guy walked over and helped me with the third one, he even offered to carry it over to his table and ask me to sit, yes indeed. He was fine, I didn't feel bad I wasn't doing anything wrong by talking to him. So after getting over my embarrassing moment with him. We talked a while and he was amazed on how shitty my boyfriend was being to me, I would never treat a lady like that, oh baby, I wanted to burst with infidelity thoughts, I thought about him and that bimbo and my reformed burger, I grabbed him by the hand and he never ask where we were going or what was going on, he just followed. We were on the dark side of the building at night and didn't even think about it just laid one on him and stepped back and apologized for being so forward and started to walk off and then we were one, we ended up over by his truck but I couldn't go that far with him. Even though I know for a fact that he has cheated on me and I still can't.

We went back inside and he bought me a beer and then the show started. My boyfriend was on top of this wall and it is slippery at night and there is water on the other side. He is a world jackass but I don't want the fool to hurt himself. He walks up and down the wall singing and plastered out of his gored. After about an hour of yelling at him to get down he leaps off the other side and I thought he's dead, I scramble to get up on the wall, the guy I met helped me he was also concerned, and there on the other side he has laying on the beach making sand angels, I forgot that the water didn't go all the way up the wall. That was wrong to do that to people. I walked off and went back to the bar where his truck was, kissed him and said by. He said leave with me, I will take care of you. Boy did I want to go but again there's that annoying voice again stay with stupid. I went back to the beach and sat right where everything started.

## THE END

# THE AWH MOMENT

One day I made a trip down to where they lived and I thought that I would bring a little green with me. It wasn't much, just enough to catch one buzz. But it was very powdery so I had to be careful with it. I got on the bus and I was out of here. My dad was going to pick me up at the bus station where they live. I got there he picked me up and we headed back to the one room motel. I never told my dad that I smoked but I don't think that he was very stupid.

I got there and one of my sisters were there and I asked her if she wanted to catch one, so we strolled outside around the back of the motel where we can have a little more privacy. The 6 inches, grass out back made a good cover. I got out a rolling paper and poured the stuff oh so carefully, I didn't want to waste a drop. I poured it in the paper no sweat, I start to roll the jay, and a gust of wind comes by and blows all the stuff off of the paper and into the tall grass, no, no, no.

Well I guess god didn't want me to have that, I get it but dam he could of at least I had the thing rolled, that's was cruel and cold. Now you see me and now you don't.

THE END

# THE CHICKEN HUSBAND

I lived in a rather large town, in this hole of an apartment I lived in, Why can't I every live in something nice, Maybe one day just not now. I had a son and a daughter, she was a little younger than her brother. One day I called her father and asked him if there was some way that he could bring me some diapers for is daughter. He just hung up on me. Oh well I guess I am not getting those diapers. I would have bought them myself but all my money was tied up in rent for this hole I live in.

My first husband was just that, not the best crayon in the box. But He was the one that got me away from the one that I needed diapers from. This man came with the diapers, and he was not happy to see my old man holding his daughter. He got very mad and took his daughter from him. Than he managed to, assault, him. My old man takes off into the apartment I thought that he was going to get something to help me get this guy from hurting me, because, at the time he was assaulting me. He hears sirens coming and he lets go of me and takes off. The officials show up and I tell them my problem and they just say;

Call us if he comes back. I look at him in amazement. The next time you will be called is when I am dead.

I had wondered where in the hell did my husband took off to. I went in the apartment and the kitchen window was open. This window is only 10 inches high and about 20 inches long and this man was ne skinny Minnie. He about 200 pounds and he squeezed out of that window, instead of helping me and my family, our family I thought. I know that the cop situation has improved greatly over the years but they still should have done something. Never count on them all the time because they can't be everywhere all the time.

## THE END

# CHRISTMAS TREE PARKING

I was with my second husband, my son. One day my father in law had to have his annual checkup at a hospital and he asked if we could take him. Sure, he was a very up there, let's just say he as old as a dinosaur. He out lived 3 wives. One of them being my mother.

The trip was long. We, my father in law, mom, my husband and me. It was a hot day. We got about a half a mile before we got to the hospital, we broke down, right in the middle of making a left turn at a three way. Oh, just fantastic. We pushed the car in to an empty Christmas lot. Thank god it wasn't Christmas because the lot would be full and it would be colder than a well diggers ass. Been there done that, no thanks. We looked to see what was wrong, while we were doing that my father in law walked to the hospital for his appointment.

I still don't understand why mom had to come, she didn't walk to the hospital with him so what was the purpose. When we were at the light the car hit the ground when we tried to make that left turn. It was the drive axel. We started working on the car, the bad axel had to come out so we could find another one. While all of this is going on mom is in the car just bitching up a storm, like she has turret syndrome. What is it? I'm hot, I'm thirsty, I'm hungry, I got to pee. Well so does everybody else. You should have stayed home. You are now with your husband that is at his appointment. Why didn't you go with him? Ai don't want to walk, well you are going to have to wait and see. My husband was walking up the road to a gas station to see if he can get some help.

Mom and I are trying to find a place go pee, but we were at a crossroad, one small building that's no bigger than a taco stand, not much cover to do what we had to do, so it was you pee I keep watch for cars. My husband came back and said that he called everyone in my family but they are all as poor as church mice. Than he called his mom and she could help us but not for a couple of days. All day we sat with our feet hanging out of the window, trying to attract attention without getting arrested. Nobody would stop.

Now we are stuck here for a few days. It started getting dark and time to sleep, we wanted my mom to sleep in the back and him and I sleep in the back because of the steering wheel. But no, she fought us tooth and nail on that one and we lost. It was already a day from hell, and now I sleep with a steering wheel jabbed in my ribs, we struggle all night. The son started coming up and the car was getting hot. Dam no coffee, no water, no food. I am thinking to myself, thank god again, that I didn't have my son here. He is safe home with, with his aunt. Plus, he did want to go but when I mentioned it was a place where they stick people with needles, he was all too happy to stay with her.

That next day was brutal, when we thought is there any hope? Afar in the distance, there was a construction site, it was a good distance away, but for some reason, we see something that we didn't see before. A port-a-potty. A beautiful sight. I said mom is that what I think it is, I should have never opened my mouth. We scrambled out of the car so fast that it looked like we were in a race for a million. We ran for what seemed forever. We get to it, what a sight, it was real, the place was very muddy and this port-a-potty was sitting on a little hill, up away from the construction. she jumps ahead of me and gets to it first. Me first, fine, and when I let go of the door on the port-a-potty, and this thing had a big ass spring on it and when I let go of the handle, and this thing started to teeter like a bowling pin, oh my god I hope this thing doesn't topple over. Not that that wouldn't be funny as hell. But her getting hurt, no I definitely, didn't want her to get hurt. Now this thing sways back, but lands back down, that was a close one. She swore I did that on purpose, I told her that I didn't and if I was going to do that I would have waited until you were in it than push it over the hill. That just happened, in my favor. Probable paying you back for the sleeping arrangements. That evening, just before dark a car pulled up, it was a guy that just happen to be driving what we were. This gentleman was retired. He asked us if there was anything he could do for us. He took my husband up to get the part for the car. When they returned the guy had sandwiches, coffee, and water. We thanked him for all of his help. We started working on the car, it took a while to fix and it was getting dark and we didn't have any light to work with. We had to close up shop for the night, back to the steering wheel in the ribs.

That night was real chilly and we had no blankets with us. This guy comes back and brought us warm coffee and blankets. What a saint' maybe my dad looking out. He said that was all he had at is house, he had the sweet lady with him. We didn't care we were happy that he even bothered to stop at all. We get the car fixed and thanked the guy for everything and we were on our way, three days, stuck in a car with my lovely mother. We all needed a shower.

We picked up my father in law and he said that they took very good care of him while he was in there, he asked us what happened to us for three days. We got home safely and never made that trip again. Always carry supplies with you. Blanket, pillow, water, crackers, change of clothes and a dam flashlight.

## THE END

# THE MISSING BATTERY

My son and I lived in this place where there were woods, pine trees, Tall as the eye can see. The was this national falls' that I lived always from but you could hear it at night. There was a brook by our home. This place was pretty. My sister lived just down the road with her husband. One day it was snowing for a while, then it started hailing. Like it had nothing else better to do than to hail on my parade.

My sister and her husband wanted to go out of town for a while and wanted to know if I wanted to go, sure, drag the kids out at night, dress them, then winterize them, in the middle if a storm. Crazy or what?

But he wore me down, I gave in. Packed in a hurry, and we were off. We got about 5 miles and the car dies. No lights, no horn, no nothing, it's because he buys cheap shit and that's what happens, nothing. Everything is dead, just like I wanted to do to him at that moment. My sister and I get elected by him to go to the house and get the other battery out of the other car and carry it back, are you kidding me? That thing is heavy. I am thinking, you, lazy dog, a dog would go. Oh, my back. We walked back to the house, the snow was about a couple of inches thick and it is slippery than snot underneath. We get there and he had another car there, we had to get the battery out of this thing, we open the door and pull the hood latch and the hood would not open. We banged on it, and it was starting to get darker and colder. I said well, I will go up underneath the hood and get the battery out that way. Good idea. I laid in the snow and the ice and it take me a minute, the ground was hard and crunchy, and the front of the car was low. I got under it and managed to get my arm up un the compartment where the battery is and there is no battery there. She says what do you mean there is no battery in there. I'm feeling where the battery is supposed to be and it isn't there, just air. After no solution, we headed back. By this time, we are twice as cold, and have no battery, and I am all wet now, to add to the already bad situation, and on top of all that, utter rage. The walked helped cool me down. We got back to the car and told him that there wasn't a battery in the car. He says oh yea I took it out and put it in this one. What a bone head. Now we all got to walk back to the house again. Double check everything before you leave.

## THE END

# THE BLIND BIRTHDAY

O ne of my best friends and her husband, came over to my house, so the guys could gab and the girls do whatever we do. She asked me out of the blue if I ever been to a casino, no, do you want to go? Sure, but I don't have any money. You don't have to worry about that, ok. I went, it took us about 40 minutes to get there. We did not have one of these where we lived. We got inside of this place. It was bright, all the bells going off, the chips hitting the table, gadgets and gizmos. She gave me 20 dollars wow that lasted a whole 5 minutes. We walked around for a while. Had a couple of drinks. She suggested we go to eat some lobster. Now you know I can't afford that, let me guess you got this, she was almost like one of my children, because she is smaller than me. We help each other, be there when you need them, no matter what, and a lot older, so I felt like her elder.

The meal was fantastic I had never eaten lobster before. We had the tall drinks. After the great meal, we headed home, this was fun we will have to do this again. She stopped at a little mart to get some gas and when she got in the car she told me that she wanted me to do something for her without saying anything, no questions asked. I paused for a moment and said okay, but was a little slow to answer. I agreed. She pulled a mask out of her hand bag and said put this on. Now wearing the mask is one thing but it had power puff eye balls on it, big ones. I started to laugh, you, kidding me. You promised me. Yes, I did, and put it on. I felt like an idiot with big eyes. Now how I looked was another whole thing. She starts to drive and hope that I lose my sense of direction and I won't know where she was taking me. She turned up streets and down them, she would go through parking lots, I could hear some people and cars than traffic. Than we would stop. This went on for about 10 minutes. She stops the car and she tells me to wait before I get out. I know that she had a brother that lived close by and from the way she was going was there. She thinks she has got me fooled, except this stupid thing on my face. She takes me out of the car by the arm, leads me through sticker bushes, pot holes, small bushes. After a few minutes I could hear music, then I thought a bar, oh my god I am going to be so embarrassed, being caught with this thing on my face. She rips the mask off, and I stand there looking like an idiot. Everybody was there, decorations, and I was in my own garage. Everyone yelled surprise! I was surprised. Floored. She got me on that one. Love you See it goes to show you, you, don't know everything. I had a really good time.

***

# THE ROLLOVER

lived I a small town. Can't afford to live in a big one. I lived with my mom, my friends and I thought that we should go riding around and decided to go drive somewhere. They will be having a parade down town, this was always a big deal to these people around this part of town, to me it is ok I have seen it quite a few times. There was a guy driving and my girlfriend and another friend. We wanted to go somewhere else and do something else. We set off out of town. We did not know what we wanted to do, so we drove for a while and some dumb ass says why don't we go horseback riding. Not at no 10am in the morning, it was foggy and just nasty. The guy driving, turns the car around in someone's grass and says that he is going back to town and pick up someone else, so we turned around and headed back and we were driving about 40 and he came upon this turn in the road, been around it a million times and he took the turn normal.

This turn was on a quite high hill than tappers off as the turn straightens out. We made half of the turn and the car slit off the road. I rolled about 3 times than it rolled from nose to nose, then finally rolling one more time. When we were done we were upside down, and facing the other way, and I was no longer in the back seat I was in the front and everybody else was in the back of the car. My head hit the back window of the car and my head hurt. I could see my girlfriend and she was all upside down, folded all up. She moved and that was good. The other two started making noises of pain from the accident, that was a good sign, if they are in pain then they are alive. I could smell gas, that was not a good sign. We scrambled out of the car. It was starting to smoke, better hurry. We got out and crawled to the top of the hill. By that time there was an ambulance there, I guess someone called them. I helped my girlfriend out. My mouth had glass in it. My mouth was very crunchy. I crawled to the top of the hill and when I did I was facing the ground and the first thing that I see is a little pair of shoes, caught me off guard. I looked up and with a little chuckle and a sorry right after. There was a midget paramedic, it was funny at first, because I never saw one for real, I thought that they were tv. He said that he gets that a lot and not to worry about it, and asked if I was ok, I had hurt myself at mom's house with a knife (another, story) back a while before this accident and I had stiches in my hand and it had already had a bandage on it, really, do you think that I bandaged it in the car as it was rolling over. We were taken to the hospital and treated. My girlfriend she had a bad shoulder, and the other two were banged up some.

We ended up going to the liquor store and getting some beer and going to the parade anyway. Should have stayed where we were and went to that parade.

***

# THE GIRL WITH THE RED HAIR

I lived with this guy, in this country farm with lots of room to roam. This place was ok I think the company maybe another story. It was a Friday and that means I have to put his (my, boyfriend) clothes out for his meetings he says he goes to on Fridays. It probably a meeting for, how to treat your woman shitty. I know that this is one of those days that everything sets him off. You had to be very careful what you said because the next thing you know you are clocked in the face. Most of the time I just don't say anything, I watch. One day I am sure that karma will pay him a visit.

He left the house and off to his meeting or whatever meeting it happens to be. Later he comes home and he wants to go out for the evening. This is not unusual. For me, it is, humiliate me night. I hate these, you are never going to know how it is going to go, bad, or worse. We get there in the same place I met him. We walk in and he walks over to someone he knew and leaves me standing there, Should I walk with him or just stand here, I never knew what to do ever. I'm standing there, dresses like a street walker. I did not like this, it was not me, I'm more old school. I know exactly why I am dressed that way, for people to stare at me, then he can treat me like shit later.

There was this red headed girl that came over to him, rubbing all up against him, dam near tried to get in his pants right there. I saw her around, she came to the motel a lot. Most of the time with a man in tow. Now she was up on the bar dancing for him. She had on this cocktail looking thing on and not much else, you could see all of her under carriage. This was making my blood boil, even though I rather leave this place without him would not bother me one bit, but it was the point of it. These are the little games that he would play. Look at me I can do that shit and get away with it. I know he is wanting me to go over there and say something to this bitch. Well I did. She did not like it, but he was sure loving it. Later when we were ready to leave he told me to walk over to this girl with the red hair and tell her: You might dance for the rest but he's going home with the best: I don't know what in the hell that was. As I was telling this girl what he told me to tell her, I came outside and I be dammed. There are two bimbos sitting in his truck. I don't think so. I walked over to the truck, and yanked the passenger door open and asked what are those two bitches doing in my truck where I sit? I told, the two of them, get the hell out of my truck. They got out and him sitting there with a smug look on his face. For some reason I said, really, not thinking what would happen. He said nothing. I can't wait till we are home. Than the fun begins, He accused me of sleeping with all kinds of people even though I never went out of his sight. Bed time, go put some ice on my eye, go to bed and I get to do this all over again next Friday.

Life is hard enough in this world without being used as someone else's door mat. I know this now. The more that they think that they can get away with the more they will do. My suggestion would be when he treats you like that you find a cast iron skillet, and when it happen, give him one good once over and he will not treat you like that again. If you don't stand up for yourself, no one will.

## THE END

# A SISTER'S DOWNFALL

outhern town, not too big. My older sister and my other sister that is a little younger than me. We would travel to school by bus, it was a long walk. After school, the kids would always put us on the wrong bus we would be lost and had to get the bus drivers go out of their way to take us home, this was getting out of hand. We started to walk to school every day. One day after school we said that we weren't going to take the bus home. Thank god that day my younger sister did not go to school that day, it was just my older sister and me. We wanted to walk we are not dealing with those nasty kids any more. One day we were outside getting ready to head home. One of the girls pushed my sister and she picked up a rock and threw it at her and it hit her in the head, paybacks. We headed home and we got a long ways, down the road.

We had to walk along this heavy congested highway. Not paying attention, my sister got hit from behind, someone pushed her down an embankment, into a bunch of stickers bushes, she was tangled up in them. I wanted to help her but I wanted to take care of the bitch first. The first thing I did was go see if she was ok and told her that I would be back. I'm going after her. I left and ran across this, two lane highway, when I got across the road there was this patch of woods, I found this 2x4 with rusty nails in it. That will work. It wasn't much to work with, but it will do. I was going to hit her so hard with this thing, she would have sprung a leak next time she drank something. Or better yet when she goes swimming she sinks quicker than the Titanic. I chased her for a good distance but didn't catch her. I went back to see if I could get her untangled from all those briers. I got her un done and we went home and we never saw those girls after wards. I am glad, school was bad enough without all that. There comes a point when you just can't take any more and you snap. Family is a tricky thing. You can talk about each other, behind everyone's back, but when it comes down to it, Family always stick together, talk about each other later.

\*\*\*

# PLAYING "ROB THE HOUSE"

We lived in a place way back off of the road, Life as a little, 9 year old girl, shouldn't have problems, well let me tell you. Kids hating on you at school, throwing fire crackers at us at the bus stop, making fun of me, about my last name, spitting on me. The life I had at home. Dad worked all the time and mom stays home and takes care of the kids and cleans the house. It would have been nice if she did any of that. When dad would leave for work she would change, I don't mean her underwear. She would put all of us outside and lock the door, except for my baby sister, she was still an infant. She would lock the door and around lunch tome or whenever her soaps are done than we get fed. She would open the window about 5 inched, just enough to get a loaf of bread and a gallon of water. The water would be squirting from under the cap, because she would not open the window enough to get the jug out of the window. The baby would be crying for hours and she would not even let us in to take care of her, yet she wouldn't do it.

One school days we leave like we usually do and when we get out of sight we would hide in the woods from her, we wouldn't do this all the time, most of the time it was when she would go to the store with our grandfather. She would leave with him, stop right where we were hiding. Except we were real close. We were in a tree right above her head about 200 feet up. When she would stop get out of the car and stand there and holler at us, I know you are in there come out, we just sat there and let her holler. Always when she went grocery shopping the kitchen was always left with shit that nobody wanted and we would stock our fort with it. She never caught on. We would also use her dresses they made very good hammocks to sleep in. We would sit in the woods or find something to get into. Now the homework, we would do about 1 hour of school work, so it looked like we did something, like went to school. There is nothing wrong having a fort when you are young, it shouldn't have to be your way of life.

***

# THE EMBARRASSING ENCOUNTER

I lived in a small town. Everybody knows everybody. A friend stopped by and was parting a few trailers down and wanted me to come down there. I said no thanks and refused. He leaves and comes back again and said that there was a guy down there that I would like to meet. No thanks, I really don't want to. Well he wore me down. I went down there and there were a few people there and this gut that he wanted me to meet. He was ok I guess. I had a few beers and this guy was sitting in an overstuffed chair. My friend pushes me right on top of this dude. I was so embarrassed. I got up and apologized, and walked into the kitchen. He came in and said that he was ok. We sat in the kitchen not saying a whole lot. I just said why done we go up to my place where it would be a less noise. He was ok. We grabbed the rest of the beer out of the icebox and went up to my place. My baby sister and her boyfriend were there. He comes in and sits down. I didn't bring him here for a booty call. I'm a little more dignified than that, I'll wait. I got a beer and sat down in this rocker we had, it threw me under my kitchen table. He and everybody laughed, oh it is funny that I am covered in beer. I got another beer and turned the leg on the chair so it would not do that again and I sat down, right under the table again. I got up and slammed that dam chair down and fixed that leg again. Mind you they are still laughing from the first and second one. I sat down and again right under the table. That chair went right out into the front yard. I got up and went into the bathroom to wipe the beer off of me and when I got back into the living room, he was gone. Where did he go? Nobody knew, they said that he just got up and left. I was mad that he just took off without saying anything. Later that week I was in the shower and I had my hair full if shampoo, my neighbor hollers over that I had a phone call, its him. I turned the water off and wrapped a towel around me head soap and all I ran over there as fast as I could. He said that he was sorry for leaving, without saying anything. He wanted to make a date with me, so he said I'll bring the vodka and you bring the orange juice. He said that he didn't want to laugh at me, so he left. We have been together 30 years.

\*\*\*

# TARGET SHOOTS

One day my dad had entered up into a shooting competition. It was my baby sister my older sister and dad and me. We went to one of those competitions. You can shoot whatever you want to shoot with as long as you don't use a scope. Dad had a few guns. They always sat around the house loaded. We knew what they did, we would find out the hard way. Dad would come home and if one of our toys is laying in the yard, it is open season for target shooting. He would get his little table he built and prop you up with a 22 and he would make you shoot at your toys till there wasn't anything left of them. Little tiny pieces. We learned to keep the toys out of the yard. At the competition, you had to draw numbers and when your number is up you shoot at a target that they put up for you. My father had a shotgun that had a problem with, every time you would shot it would pop open and pinch you. He wrapped the barrel and the stock with red, white, and blue electrical tape. He called it old glory. It did not look like much but it was on the money. You hit what you aim at. There were these people there shooting with high powered guns. The ones that cost an arm and a leg.

There was dad my older sister and me shooting and by the

end of the day we ended up with one whole side if pork, a couple of canned hams, a couple of bags of groceries, some cash, now sure how much dad kept that. The car was loaded and so was my father. He got in the car and we ended up in the middle of nowhere. Dad pulled off into this parking lot so he could teach her how to drive. She was scared but I know she can do this, she was 12 just barely looking over the steering wheel. A crash course in the basics. This was a stick shift, and she had no idea how to do it. Now out on the road we were. She did ok, she stalled it a couple of times. At one point, there were some people behind her beeping their horn, she would get out of the car and yell at them, you try driving a stick. Scream out of the window at them. She still did a whole lot better than dad was doing, swerving all over the road. It was enough to make me wet myself several times. She got us home. Mom was feeling generous, she let just once let us stay home from school the next day. All for the glory of food.

\*\*\*

# RUBBER EGGS

When I left home for the second time, I moved to this nice busy town. Lots of things to do. I went to visit my parents and they lived about 2 hours away from me. One weekend I went to see them and after the visit I was heading home and they did not want me to go back home. Before I left there, I was talked into coming back to live there. I did not want to live there I had a nice apartment where I was. They lived in a, two room, place, they barely had room for themselves. They said that they would watch my son for me, their grandchild. Well it would be a little easier, I could get some stuff done. I headed back to my place by bus. I got there and packed all, of my stuff. One of my biggest suitcases I had all the can goods from cub bards. And I had a paper bag with handles I put all, of the icebox stuff in. And a regular bag for the boxed items. I started to get hungry. I put 6 eggs in a crock pot and filled it with water and turned it on. I went back to what I was doing. I laid back a little to stretch my back because it was killing me, from all I did that day. I fell asleep, I woke up to this weird sound. It sounded like two kids in the kitchen playing jump rope with high heels on. I know that I don't have any high heels even in my apartment. I have

78

kids and they are not here. I got up to find out who is making all that noise in the kitchen. Here I put those eggs in that crock pot and forgot all about them. These things were jumping around in the pan, all the water had evaporated. They looked like Mexican jumping beans. I looked at the clock and I was late for my bus, I had to get a move on, Thank, god that the bus station was only a block away, I wrapped the eggs and they were scorching hot. Grabbed all what I could carry and I was gone, I will have to come back and get the rest of my things when I get the time. I locked up and ran for the bus and hope I didn't miss it. I didn't miss the bus. I got on the bus with a little difficulty, but I made it. I but the suitcase in the overhead and the bag with the icebox stuff in it. I got settled in my seat for that long ride. Half way I got hungry, I thought of those eggs. I opened the container and got one out and peeled it, it peeked so nice, that never happens. I went to take a bite of the egg and almost broke a tooth. That egg was so rubbery, if I was to bounce it inside of this bus, it would kill everybody on it. It had vulcanized. Turned to rubber. No eggs for me, great for the kids to play with, bounce it and see if you can catch it.

I finally got to the bus station, well a brick building with a sign in the window that says greyhound. The bus stopped and I got up and had to get my stuff out of the overhead. And the other stuff. Well I managed to bash some woman in the back of the head with the suitcase. When I bent down to get the bag of box goods, I caught someone else with the other bag. I better get off the bus before I kill someone. The suitcase was so heavy. I managed to get off the bus. When I took that last step, off, of the bus the bag of icebox stuff broke and my head of lettuce went rolling down the street, the peanut butter went rolling under the bus, and I had this big pad of butter wrapped in plastic and it is round and it decided to go another way. Just when I thought that my day couldn't get any worse. Yes, it can. Dad shows up in this car that sounded like a lawnmower having a bad day. It was smoking and everybody on the bus knew this one's for me. Dad would have picked me up in a horse and buggy as long as I get to my destination. Assume you're going to have a bad day and then when you do have a good day it will be worth it.

## THE END

# HUSBAND IS HOME

I live in this nice home, but it needs a little tender loving care, taking care of a home isn't easy. If you rent, you are just throwing your money right out the window. Now if you own, there anything that you put into your home is call equity, and that you get back. And you don't have people telling you what to do with your stuff. Now sometimes you have what I call a bad day, everyone has them. One year we had a small earthquake, we did feel it but faint. Right after that it started to rain, I don't mean rain I mean Noah's ark. And that's how we found out that the basement is no good for a swimming pool. The earthquake cracked the foundation and the basement was a pool. My son and I were trying to get rid of all the water. We couldn't pour it outside because the ground was already saturated already. The outside drain wasn't draining. While were down there scooping up water we heard my husband come home and walk all the way across the living room and the dining room and set his lunch pail on the table and then as usual he slams his keys on the table' My son and I heard him and quickly my son said that he will go upstairs, real, quick and get him to help us before he takes his boots off and get him to help us move these two TVs he had down there, before he gets comfortable. Once he does that's it he is done for the evening. My son runs up there yelling to him don't take your shoes off yet we need your help moving these TVs. He turns the corner and there isn't anyone there. No one. He came down stairs and I asked him if he is coming to help us? He said no, no. It will only take a minute. Mom he is not there. We both heard him. Late that da I heard my sister come in, and there was no one there. What is going on?

I know what I heard and I know what he heard. After the water went down we had to dig up our basement to fix a long, busted pipe. Homes can always be a blessing and sometimes they can be a fickle bitch. In the long run, your money is well spent buying a home.

***

# THE DOLLAR

I lived in that big city, Getting away from, other people's, drama. No, I seem to attract it. I seem to also get myself into these stupid living arrangements. I am to be living my son and me. No, I have 2 grown men fighting over a dollar. I had this apartment and I let my older sister and her husband move in. My boyfriend would drop by, once, in a while and party. They got into a little bit more than they were supposed to. They had a bad glue habit. They got into this big fight. One was saying that he gave him that dollar he promised him and the other one was saying that he already gave it to him. The fight turned into a hair pulling, knock down drag out fight. I can't have this here. Someone called the cops because, because they were knocking on my kitchen window. I have a buzzer to my apartment but they said that they rang it for a while and no one would answer. We had to hide all the empty tubes of glue, not that you couldn't smell it. I let the cops into my window because someone broke my door several weeks earlier. The cop made my brother in law open his wallet to see if he really did give him that dollar and it was still in his wallet, son he never gave it to him. Fighting over that like two, 5, year, old's. Later that night my brother in law set his bag of glue on top of my new stereo and it ate a hole in the lid. See even if you use glue you still can't hold a family together.

***

# THE DISCO WATCH

I'm still in that big city, just started my new job. I was so excited. My first paycheck. I went to the store and bought myself a digital watch, they were the rave back then. After I got the watch, we wanted to go out, maybe to a club. My brother in law was very tight when it came to spending money, everywhere we went we had to walk. One day. We wanted to go somewhere nice, we got all gussied up and we headed down the road trying to find a place to go. We walked forever and my feet were hurting and we haven't even got there yet. We found this great disco they were hosting a famous person. We went in and this place was bumping. The place was full of people dancing and disco lights were everywhere. Sore feet or not, I'm going to sit myself down somewhere and party. There was this gut there from the minute I walked in he was all over me. You want to dance, you want to go home with me. Dude I don't even know you. he became a real pain in the ass.

After about the third trip over to me, I just told him that we were real close to the hospital, and that if he keeps bothering me he will be a patient there. He left me alone. They did have the tables set up strange, like you were at a barn dance, rows of tables. A really, good, song came on and both my sister and I went out on the dance floor. I was out there with my hands in the air, getting down with my bad self. And the next thing I know, there is very angry women charging at me, maybe it was someone behind me, she gets up in my face and then snatches this wad of hair, off, of my watch. Apparently when I got up to dance I ripped her bun, off, of her head. how embarrassing for me and her. I apologized to her but she didn't want to hear it. We walked home from there and boy did I have blisters. Next time wear some comfortable shoes and change them when you get there.

***

# THE FRIENDLY BIKER

I was living with my mom for a short period of time, till I can get on my feet. I went out one night with my girlfriend to this biker party. There were bikers there and they were drinking pictures of water so I thought. They were pictures of vodka. People sitting around smoking without a care in the world. They don't care that the cops may stop by. Didn't bother them. My girlfriend and her boyfriend were doing their thing. I meet this biker. He was, really, nice, but he was a little handzy. It was time to leave and head home and he wanted to tag along. I think that he had more on his mind then a ride home. On the, ride home this gut had more hands then an octopus. I could not keep him, off, of me. It was like trying to fight off a bull. My father showed me something, I think it was time I showed him. I said to him that I wanted to play a game. You win you can do whatever you want to me, but if you lose you, have, to leave me alone. He agreed. Of course. He would think that typical man. He was about three times bigger than me, not fat but a big dude. You interlock your fingers, just like you are holding hands and squeeze. The first one to holler mercy loses. I was hoping that he didn't know the secret to it. It's not that secretive.

You just squeeze and twist at the same time, it is very painful. He hollered mercy first. He was also on his knees. I know that sounds cruel but dad taught us how to get out of situations like that. He honored the rules and he was a perfect gentleman for about one hour. He was back to the hands again. I wonder if octopus have this problem.

***

# KEEPING WARM

When in was young, we lived along this big highway. During the, day she would put all of us in a bedroom together and take a pair of pantyhose and tie the door, so we couldn't get out. No bathroom breaks, no eat breaks, no outside world. You know even prisoners get a hot meal. They get to go to the bathroom. I know there was food, because we could smell it bacon, eggs, toast, even coffee. We would get so bored there was nothing to do. We did everything three thousand times. There is got to be something to do. We climbed out of the bedroom window. It was really, high, up off the ground. Getting down was one thing but up is another. We climbed out and went through the field that was there. On the other side were these old mobile homes. To get to them we had to get past this guy sitting in a chair right in front of this big bay window. We got a kick out of it, when we would tap on the glass and duck down so he had no clue where the noise was coming from. The last time I did that I lost a patch of meat, off, of my forehead, that didn't feel too good. After that we went into one of the trailers. It was cold in the trailer. There was this cabinet there and I put some paper in it and lit it, then I was warm. But suddenly I couldn't get the flames to go out. I hurt my hand trying to do that. It was beyond my control. We got the hell out of there, ran across this field and almost got run over by a corn combine. We leaped into these small windows without even scaling the wall. We could see the smoke from the room. We sat there got out the cards and acted like we have been in there all day, and we were. After a while there was a knock at the door. It was the fuzz. They wanted to know if she or her kids seen anything, she said no and mom walked over to the door where we were and unwrapped the pantyhose from around the door knob. We came out of the room, like gaged animals, like flocks of birds. My kids have been here all day. Now what bothered me was that the cop never said anything about the pantyhose or us being locked in this room all day. Nothing. There was a little boy walking outside on the other side of the highway. The cop left and went up the road to where the boy was and picked him up. What happened to him I don't know. When the cop left, it was back in the room. Until it was time for dad to get home. The last thing I remember being in that house. One night it was late and the baby was crying. We were all sleeping in the same bed then. I got up and told mom that the baby was crying, come take care of it. She never come and the baby would not stop crying, finally I woke dad up and said something to him and he got up and came into the bedroom and turned the light on and in the bed where we were sleeping there was a rat chewing on the baby's fingers. Dad set traps that he made himself. We had to move from this place, before the rats eat all the children.

## THE END

# THE SHADOW PERSON

One night when I was young, about 9, my older sister was one year older than me. The community that we lived in was like the dark side of the moon, I say that not to offend the dark side. One night we were all in bed and a few hours had passed by, our room that we all slept in was in between the kitchen and our parents room. The moon was shining in through the kitchen window. Later I heard some rustling around in the living room. Everyone was in bed. The noise got more, loud. I tried to ignore it. Then I saw a shadow of a person in the house. The shadow looked like he was wearing a helmet. I think that they call that a, afro. I could not move I was frozen in place. I was so scared. I just laid there. He got her out of bed and they went into the other room. The next thing I know the cops were there and they were, filing, out a report for sexual assault. I felt bad that I should have helped her but I was afraid he would hurt me. The guy that assaulted her stole 21 dollars out of dad's wallet that was on the coffee table. What was strange, the guy that assaulted her gave her 20 dollars out of the 21 he stole. My sister said that exactly what he did. He said if I give you 20 dollars you don't tell the cops. She agreed but still told them. The officer said that, that was a little hard to swallow, Dad said well you can believe it. When she says that's what happened than that's what happened. Times have changed in life since I was little. Nothing was ever done.

***

# THE OLD CABBY CAR

We were Living very close to a big city. We wanted to go visit our grandmother, since grand pappy was coming to our house to see dad and hang out with him, play poker, smoke cigars, drink whatever they can get their hands on. We had a nice stay. We headed home and on the way home the car we were in broke down. We were on the side of the road and it was about 50 degrees. We sat there for hours and sang songs, and did whatever we had to, to keep from freezing to death. This was one of those times when mom was being a good mom. She even opened a bottle of wine that grand pappy left in there. She would give us a capful about every 30 minutes. Normally mom wouldn't have given a rat's ass if we froze to death, but something was in her that night. Finally, I got out of the car and between mom and myself we got the hood open. The air was cold and it was dark and we were in the middle of nowhere. There wasn't any traffic. Looking under the hood we had no idea what we were doing or what to do and no phone to call anyone for help. Mom said we needed to find a phone booth but the only thing we could see was a school and some woods, but no phone. In the far distance we could see lights, not many but maybe a phone at least. Guess who got elected to walk the highway and hope there was a pay phone. I headed up the highway, I was scared, and I was all by myself. I would have done it anyway, it was either that r freeze to death. There was a phone next to the gas station that was closed down, so I called dad. By that time dad and grand pappy were drunk but still awake. I told him we were broke down. He asked what the car did and I told him that it just died. He said it was probably the battery or the alternator. He said to go back to the car and do a few things to see of it was the battery or something else. So I walked back to the car which took about 20 minutes, and mom said what did your father say. He said to try to start the car and pull the positive cable off of the battery and if the car quits running it's the alternator. So we tried to start the car and it wouldn't turn over, so I walked back up the street to the pay phone to call dad back. I told him what was going on. Dad was more worried about me and if we were okay. I told him we were okay but that we were cold, hungry and sleepy. By this time, I looked like a grease monkey. Dad told me to go back to the car and try something else, back to the car I go again. Dad said if the car didn't start it could be the battery and that there was a battery in the trunk that we could put jumper cables on to start the car. But guess what, there weren't any cables. Mom said to go call dad again. I said hell no I wasn't going to do that a third time. I took the battery out of the trunk and I turned it upside down onto the negative and positive post and had mom crank the car and what do you know the car started. I don't know why the car died, but at this point I didn't care. Mom slammed the hood we all hopped in the car and shot out of there like a bat out of hell. We go about 50 miles and the car died again, except this time we were almost home but not quite home. We were next to a pay phone this time and called dad, and told him that we were broke down again, and the extra battery wouldn't work the second time. So grand pappy got in his car and him and dad came and got us. The car had a bad alternator. I do know that when I turned the battery upside down the liquid burned holes in my pants. I guess this is what they mean when they say live and learn, but I gave something a try and it worked.

## THE END

# FAIR DAY

This was an interesting day. It started out by getting out of bed, and right there is where I went wrong that day. After I got my son fed and outside to play with his cousin, and those two were the trailer park menace. They weren't bad, but would get into things, like two young boys would do. They swung on the cable cord so that it drooped so low it's hanging on the ground. The wind was kicking up and the boys said that a hurricane came through, and that's why the cord was hanging down like that, this was their excuse. I said yes, I know which two hurricanes did it. They laughed, and I knew they were swinging on it. Due to that everybody's cable went out, of course we told the cable guy a storm did it, well moving on. My brother in law came outside to talk to me, and asked me if I wanted to work at a fair. 90% of the time I wouldn't believe a word he said, never liked the man, but he was my sister's husband, but that was it. I never liked him because he was a pig in my eyes, it means he was mean to her and treated her like crap, but the fair job was on the up and up, meaning it was paid work. So, I went with my sister and her family to the fair to do a job selling tickets. You get to stand in one of them hot booths, roasting your ass off, but I made $60 bucks for working about 8 hours, so we stopped and got something to eat. It was a hot day, so when my brother-in -law stopped earlier he filled his cooler full of beer, so he can drink them all in front of me, without even offering me one. I know that's hard to believe, but this man was so tight, his wallet would scream every time he took it out. The man would put $2 worth of gas in his car at a time, no matter how far he had to travel. Even when you go to a fast food place, it would be him, my sister and their three kids in the back seat. He would order food, for example he would get two value meals, he would eat one and his wife and kids share the other. I've seen him give his wife's dinner to the dog, I could go on, but you get the idea, so on with the trip. We were on our way back home, it was about 10pm, well about 20 miles from home the car gets a flat tire on the,back passenger side. Well first we got to get the car off the road. We get out the jack, start loosening the lugs nuts and after breaking them loose, my brother -in-law gets the jack under the car and jacks the car up, so far so good. He gets the spare out of the trunk and the mother is flat as a pancake. My brother-in-law at this point who I call "Mr. Idiot" says no it isn't, so we put it on the car, let down the jack, of course it's flat. We jack it back up so we can get it to a gas station to put some air in it, and hope it's just low on air from sitting in the trunk. We take the tire off and Mr. idiot didn't block the car from rolling forward seeing we were on a small hill. Well the next thing I know the car rolls backwards and falls on top of the bumper jack. Now it's laying on the jack and he doesn't have another one. After that we sit in the car while he drinks a cold one,and I was so thirsty I could have drank urine, but he was guarding those beers like a momma bear guarding her cub, he wouldn't even give me one. After a while a cop stops to see if we needed any help, so Mr. Idiot told him what happened. Him, the family and the flat tire left with the cop to get the tire fixed. He was going to go to the house and drop his family off, and have the cop take him to the gas station, or find someone to help him. He had another car at the house so he could have come back, but he was so stingy that he would of not wasted $2 worth of gas to come back to get us, he would find someone else to run him up the road. Well my son and I had to sit in this cold car freezing our asses off. There was a cardboard windshield protector on the floor, so I covered my son with it, so it would help keep the cold from him. I sat in this car all night, and the only thing I had on my side was this cooler of cold beer. I was surprised that he didn't take it with him, what a shock and his lose. I sat in that car for hours, my son freezing. It was warm during the day, but where we were it was really cold at night. I kept a tire iron in my hands, and I drank all his beer. I didn't care, he left me and a child alone on a dark part of the highway, where semis would barrel by and shake the car really hard. It was about 4 hours that had gone by, and it was 4am. I fell asleep and woke up to this annoying beeping. I sat up in the seat and you would not believe it, in the 30 or so miles of highway right where we are, broke down, there were construction crews working on the road, or the guard railing, not really sure. I had a little hangover, and the sun coming through the window was cooking me a little. I got out of the car and one crew worker asked me if I could move, because I was in their way. I explained to him that my brother in law took the tire up to get it fixed and didn't come back, he left us. I told the gentleman that the tire was flat, and the other tire we had was flat as well. The man had a forklift or something like that and lifted the car up to get the jack from under it. The guy put air in the other tire that was flat that came out of the trunk, I thought cool just what I needed. The guy took the pumped up tire and tried to put it on the car, and what do you know, it won't go on because the lug, holes didn't match up with the lug bolts, great what next. Well all's not lost, the guy took the rim and took a torch and cut the hole until it finally fit on the bolts properly. The guy says okay now you can be on your way. Well no I can't, because Mr. Idiot took the car keys with him, now I don't have no keys DAMN DAMN crap what now. Well on Mr. Idiot's dashboard there were a dumpster of papers, chicken bones, gum, keys, receipts, dried French, fries, and I even had a dried hot dog roll over my shoulder from the back dashboard on the way to the fair, but there was a bundle of crap. I did remember he had somewhere in all this crap, a set keys, but did they go with the car, I will soon find out. God be with me, help me find one key that works in this piece of shit. What do you know, I found one key that fit, well it went in the slot, now weather it will turnover, nobody know's. The moment of truth, I turned the key and she turned over "hurray". We can go home and find out where in the hell Mr. Idiot took off to, and why he never came back. We drove for about 35 miles to get home. I get to Mr. Idiot's place, and don't even knock, I just walked in, he was lying in bed sleeping, of course when I slammed the front door, it jolted him out of bed. I yelled at him, and asked him why did you leave us stranded and didn't even bother to return. You come home and go to bed, without one ounce of care as to the two people you left stranded in your junk. He had nothing to say at all nothing. By all means' I should have kept the car, because he abandoned it, but this car was a rolling dumpster, you could see the road through the floor, when you sat in either seat. I left mad and stormed out. For reasons such as this, is why we never got along and so shall you find out, ta ta for now.

## THE END

# THE LAKE BAR

The small town where we lived there was not much to do at nights unless your're willing to drive 20 or so miles. My sisters and I had planned to go out all week, we couldn't wait. Our friend was going to be our driver, since we didn't have wheels or a driver's license. We wanted to go to this place out at the lake, we talked all week about going dancing. My dad was a stickler when it came to grades. A's were good, B's and below average were grounds for grounding and a long speech about how important it is to have a good education, and E's were the firing squad. At 16 all it sounded like was blah, blah, blah, education blah, blah, blah, good job, blah, blah, blah, make good money and on and on. All we were interested in was partying. I got pretty good grades, but all weren't up to par, but dad grounded us and said we couldn't go the dance club, and yes, he did know we were going, you don't do much without dad finding out. When he knew where we were then we could enjoy ourselves better, knowing we got permission to do so. Not this night, we just happen to get our report cards 2 days before we were going out, go figure, and they were not making dad very happy. The more cards he read the madder he was getting. He does have a rule that any A's are money, so he would give you $5 for every A you had. I always had A's in German and Math, that always got me $10 bucks, but the rest was a little iffy. I couldn't say much about the other kids, I just grabbed my money and got the hell out of the line of fire. Our friend called us and said that she was going out and asked if we were still going out, and we told her that dad grounded us. How long are you grounded for? She finally talked us into going out, it really sucked, because we really wanted to go out, been planning it all week. Schools out, the weekends here and we are grounded. No, this time we are going against dad's rules, he'll never know, we will be at the lake which is 20 miles from my house, and we'll be back home before he gets up in the morning. In secret we got all guessed up, high heels, make up, clothes that will hopefully catch us a guy's eye. Dad and mom went into their room about 9pm, and as our room was right next to theirs, we had to be very quiet while leaving. We told our friend to park a block away from the house so dad couldn't hear her, because her car was a little loud. The time was here, we crept quietly down the stairs, and out the door, and met our friend down the road. We got to the lake bar, this place I've never been before, so I'm glad we have a ride back home. Well later in the evening a couple of guys we knew were dancing and drinking with us and having a good old time. It seemed things were really going too good. It was about 11pm and we were all sitting around this large table, well guess who walks in? Dad and mom, what were the odds of that? Now that I think of it, and I never realized it until now as I sit here writing, that mom probably told dad we were out here. Now that I think of it she did it out of spite, because that bitch is just that way. I know what you're thinking, that's your mother, your loving mother, but as you will find out, if your're willing to read the rest of my books what she is all about. They showed up and were standing between the open doors arm in arm, and I elbowed my sister in the ribs, she snaps at me "what' I say look at the door, she almost choked on her drink. She elbowed my other sister and we all sat there with our mouths hanging open. The guys didn't have any clue as to what was going on. Dad looked in our general direction and if looks could kill, we would have all been dead. He walked over to the table and stared at us for about a minute or so, he opened his mouth just about to speak and the waitress came over and asked dad what she could get him, he said a Wall banger and keep them coming. Him and mom sat down, and he still didn't say anything to us, all he did was stare, a very, very uncomfortable stare. His Wall banger came to the table and he drank it down without any hesitation. At this time, we were still sitting there in amazement that he was there still staring. He drank Wall banger's all night, we went back to what we were doing, mom never said anything to us either. The night went on as if they weren't there. Our friend was there but she left about midnight, and said she would be back around 2am to pick us up. She has done that before except the last time she left me behind, and I hope this is not a repeat of that night. Mom and dad left about 12:30am, he just said see you at home, and we knew what that meant, firing squad. It sounds so harsh but it was tough love. We didn't like being punished for this or anything else, but it was better than the non-caring mom that we had. To us it was attention I guess, something to hold onto. Come closing time no friend as usual, we had no ride home. We made a few calls and managed to find a friend of a friend who just happened to be in the area, we had to pack in like sardines, but we got home okay. Do you know dad never said a word to us, ever. Thank God for the Harvey Wall banger.

THE END

# FREEZE SHACK

My son and I moved into a trailer, the landlord was such a nice man, well that was just a façade. When we moved in, we never really checked to see if everything would be working properly. I was just lucky to have a roof over my head. We moved in and just down the ways my sister who lives with her husband who is a clear ass. It was warm when we moved in but didn't need heat until we got chilly and tried to turn on the furnace, and of course no heat came out, it didn't even come on. On top of that we had no running water, or a way to flush the toilet, which I found out that the trailer didn't even have a septic tank going to the toilet which was more of a flower pot than a toilet. It wasn't even hooked to the floor or hooked to any water pipes, so of course there wasn't any water going to the trailer. From the time I moved in there, I noticed the water right off and the toilet the first time we tried to use it. I called the land lord and he didn't give a damn about anything. I called for some legal help to see if they could help us, it wasn't healthy or hygienic not to have running water or a way to go to the bathroom. I wouldn't have cared if it was just me, but I have a son to worry about. I can't live in this, it wasn't healthy at all, and we were about to freeze to death. After calling for legal help, they told me that they would check on it. I had no phone so I had to get info back by mail or I could call back. While I wait, I, have to go down to the creek, which is about 20 feet from the trailer to get my freezer items in the snow, and icebox stuff in the water, so it doesn't spoil. Winter time made it easier for icebox stuff, because I didn't have electric for a short time, so everything went to the creek so I could keep it cold or frozen. During the warm month's it was a challenge to keep food cold. After calling for legal help, my land lord's wife, a very large woman, she's trotting threw the snow with a kerosene heater. She knocks on the door and gives me this heater for the trailer, only one little thing of gas, which wouldn't get us 12 hours of heat. I still have no running water, and according to the, legal advice, I had received that told me that since I had a kid I needed to have running water. My dishes would all stick together because after I would wash them after hauling water up from the creek, before you had time to dry them they would freeze together. Good news he finally bought up a septic tank come spring, and set it in my front yard, and that's where it remained the entire time I lived there. Spring time is here, tired of burning that stinky kerosene heater, so now we are warm, somewhat. Tired of pooping and peeing in a, 5, gallon bucket. Did that for, a number of, years, finally he put in water, yeah. Now if he could hook it up to the bathroom it would be great. Now all I had to do is move, I think that is my best bet. Just because the grass is plush and green doesn't mean that there's any good dirt below it. We can call that sod, sometimes you had to live in some of the awkward places, just to live or survive.

## THE END

# NOT MY HUSBAND

Winter, cold as a blue bitch. I don't care for it myself, it was so hard to keep it warm in the house, that was here at the turn of the century, they were built in the 1920's before the depression. We were buying two homes because it was a deal, buy one house for $42000 get one free. Really it was more like 2 houses for a small payment of $48000 for both homes. The in-law home which was the extra house was a lot smaller, but anyway we decided to go for it. They looked good, what did we know, 2 houses for a real small amount. Looked good, oh yeah, tell me it isn't so, well it is. As we lived in the larger home the smaller one was livable, but we couldn't get it warm inside. The house was only 12X24 and had a brand new furnace in it, very small, my sister and her husband lived in the smaller one, and my husband and I lived in the larger one. It had 2 bedrooms, 1 bathroom, a good size living room, and a large kitchen except right in the middle of the kitchen was a chimney. You couldn't have a table in the kitchen unless it had a square hole in the middle of it. The part of the kitchen that was open enough to put a table, there was a furnace grate about 4x5, this thing was real big. The steps going up to the bedrooms was only about 6 inches wide so us having 10 and 12 size feet made it real hard to climb them, you had to walk sideways on your toes, it made it hard to get up them. The bedrooms were okay size, and it had enough windows. Not paying any attention the house seemed gloomy, and after living there, a while the house wasn't heating right either, the furnace that you could see through the grate, looked like something from world war II. It has a good foot size crack in it that someone welded or put some kind of bonding,stuff on it, don't really know, but little by little the house even had a weird smell. We never really paid any attention to it because we were in and out of the house. We went into the basement and noticed a large plate size hole in the furnace pipe that leads up to the house, we still didn't pay any attention to it, we didn't know what to do, we called the realtors, but nothing ever came of it. Life went on and one day my sister and her husband and my husband decide to go outside and smoke a cigarette. I was calling places trying to get them to help us with our situation. I tried the utility company but no go, they couldn't have given a rat's ass, who gives a shit if we don't have any heat, but we do have a large heater that doesn't work right. I hung up with the utility company, my husband walked back in because he was cold and needed his jacket. I almost had a heart attack, his lips were spotted with pink spots, and that it made him feel better by going outside. When I called the utility company back and asked them if we could get a new furnace free, I meant if there was a program where people help you out, especially during the cold season. They told me that there's nothing again that they could do. I told her that I smelled gas or something like that, almost an exhaust smell, but faint. The house also was putting off black soot, but living in the house we really didn't notice it until the soot was getting in the microwave, the refrigerator and strangely in the light switches because they had this black burst out from under the switch plate. I told them I smelled something and what should we do. Before hanging up they told me to open all the windows. Now it's January 21st, 2002, it was cold, about 2 foot, of snow on the ground, wind was whooshing through the house, we were all sitting there with our coats on. They said they would send someone to check the problem. A tech knocked at the door and came in with one of those meters to check co2. He walked through the living room, the meter beeped a little, then he walked into the kitchen where the large grate was, then all of a sudden, the meter started beeping a little louder, then the guy opened the basement door and his meter went nuts. Within 5 minutes all hell broke loose. The tech immediately told us to get out of the house, he didn't ask nicely, he said everybody "OUT NOW", he made us go outside. The next thing I know 2 fire trucks, and 2 ambulances show up, damn I didn't know it was that bad. Well immediately they took my husband into one ambulance and took him right to shock trauma, my brother in law was put into the other ambulance and whisked him away to shock trauma, another ambulance shows up, and my sister and I were trying to get in it, but I wanted to drive my car to the hospital, but the police officer that showed up along with the fire trucks told me I had to or he would put me under arrest if I didn't. I got in and they were putting oxygen on my sister and was trying to put some on me, but I was having a little problem. It was about 2:30pm and I had to get a boy from school at 3:30pm because I watched him during the day while his mom was at work. I was agitated at the EMT because he wanted to put an oxygen mask on me and I was on the phone trying to get someone to get the boy from school. So finally, the EMT puts the mask on me, the trip to shock trauma was very bumpy, the driver apologized for the rough road, we didn't care, we enjoyed it. We got to the hospital and had to walk in because they couldn't find any wheel chairs for us. We walked in the ER area and were directed to a room to lay in the bed that was there. My sister and I were together in a room, and I asked out loud I wonder where my husband was, because he came up before us. My sister says there he is, I looked and,said "that's a black man" and she said no it's not that's your husband. He had so much soot on him from that house I thought he was a black man. After about an hour of blood testing, and cleaning so we could get the soot off our skin, and some warm clothes, I went over to help my husband wipe down his body, he was the worst of all. The doctor came in and told us that we had $CO_2$ poisoning. My sister and I were the ones that had the least in our system, but my sister's husband was worse. Now my husband according to the doctor told him that if there was 30 parts of $CO_2$ in a body that was death, he had a reading of 28 parts of 30, he escaped death. Then all 4 of us had to sit in a hyperbaric chamber for a couple of hours. Just about an hour into it my sister's husband,starting having chest pains and had to be removed and have leads put on him so they can read his heart rate while being in the chamber. After all of that, that extra oxygen felt real good, I never knew how pure oxygen can feel, it's a trip. We were checked out of the hospital and was told that we might have memory loss. After all that we ended up moving in a house that the realtor was working on to sell, so we moved in it, he never did anything to rectify the problem. I want to think that my dad was looking out for us that day, and I hope that he continues to do so.

## THE END

# I GOT THE POINT

My husband and I lived in a trailer park. Not too bad a place, but I think the trailers are too close together. These trailers were so close together that I could put something on a yardstick and be able to reach the window of the other trailer and that's standing inside of the trailer. On one occasion, my sister came over cause she was more inclined to fix things. All of us have a talent of some kind fixing objects that are broken. Me myself I am more of an engine in a car kind of gal. Now don't get me wrong there is more I can fix, but this is more her department. My air conditioning duct work was broke, and my yard is about the size of a postage stamp, when the grass needed to be cut I could do it with a pair of scissors, which at the moment, needed it really bad. My sister was under the back part of the trailer and she asked me to get her the tool bag out of the car, so I did. Her tool bag had an array of different tools. I set her tool bag down in the grass and was handing her tools when she needed them. Now, why I don't know but all of her tools were sitting in the tool bag upside down, with the sharp ends of the tools sticking straight up, why I can't understand but we are talking about my sister, sometimes she's a little backwards,

109

but when I sat back to get her another tool, that I don't see here in the bag, because it got moved, so she could get to the tools easier when I wasn't there, because I had to get in the house to help her, but when I leaned back to get her another tool and somehow managed to sit back on one of her screw drivers and it went in my left butt cheek about 2 inches, it did not feel good at all. I pulled it out, after hollering for ten minutes on why she has her tools sticking up like that, then went in the house to fix my wounds. The grass was so high I didn't see the objects sticking out of the bag, I guess I should have cut the grass. The AC duct was fixed, at least we got that fixed. I'm glad she's handy, she's good at what she does, just not in organizing a tool bag.

\*\*\*

# THE VIEW

y sister and her boyfriend lived in West Virginia, a lot of back roads for four wheeling. One weekend we decided to pack up the car and head up to their place to have a cookout. Everybody was there, my family and a bunch of other family and friends. We ate, we partied the first night, she had a pool table in her dining room where her table should be, but luckily her kitchen was big enough for her to put the table in, and had a large yard for the kids to roam. The next day after everybody has gotten over their hangovers and fixed breakfast for everyone we all went four wheeling. Well my sister's boyfriend had a truck with four wheel drive, we needed to go to the store for more beer, the was on store out there that sold alcohol. After getting the beer and stuff, we decided to ride up and down back roads for fun. Pot holes, and twigs sticking out and slapping you in the face or in the back of your head. My sister was standing facing the cab, the rest of us sat down in the bed of the truck, except the one who was driving. Every time a bush would go by it would slap me in the head and no one would tell me when they would come so it wouldn't hit me, but they got more of a kick out of the bush slapping me, not funny.

The driver hit a big dip in the road and my sister had a full beer and when he hit that rut in the road her chest which was very large, that was the one thing she had going for her, so when he hit that bump her chest squeezed the beer can flat and all the beer went right in her face, that was a good laugh, laugh at me will you. We came upon an old house up on the hill, it was tattered, windows broken, big old two, story, house. Everybody wanted to go up there and see it. He drove the truck up along this road as far as possible, everybody jumped out of the truck except me, my sister and niece, only because she didn't have any shoes. I offered her mine even though they were 4 sizes too big for her feet, but she wore them anyway. My sister stayed to pee and finish her beer, not sure in that order. I had to pee also so I thought I could climb off the passenger side fender well and use the tire for a step, so I took the tissue I had in my bra, my bra was the one stop shopping for me only, but I happen to have tissue on me. I put it in my mouth and started to climb out of the truck, I put one foot on the tire, now his truck has these very large tires 4x4 so it was very high off the ground. What I didn't know was when I stepped down there was nowhere to step down to. I thought there was ground, nope not, I rolled off the side of the truck and almost down this steep hill. I got lucky and managed to grab these bushes with thorns on them, they are keeping me from falling down this ravine. I am trying to yell at my sister who was laughing at me, I'm yelling or trying to scream at her to help me and to stop laughing at me, but all that came out was "LSOLUAVIGHEFU ... OOW UH ... ... you get the picture. She is still laughing at me, the branches are snapping and their snapping fast, I'm screaming like a mad woman, but muffled. She finally helped me up, and I didn't need to go to the bathroom anymore, I'll hold it. She gets out of the truck still laughing at me managed to muster undressing so she could take a leak, that wasn't fair, but when she was done she starts laughing at me again, and she was laughing so hard she fell over right into her own pile of urine, how ironic. Everybody came back from that old house and he drove some where else up a hill, bumps, bushes, and potholes that were not helping my bladder. He stopped along some dusty road, nothing around but trees, I jumped out and decided to pee in front of the truck, because it was so high up off the ground, the hood came up to my shoulders, so I didn't have a problem about anybody seeing me, not even the ones on the back of the truck. He also had these chrome poles that were about 2 feet tall, I guess they are for aerial antennas, but they were real good to hold the toilet paper while you pee. The perfect spot, so I pull down my pants and right before I got ready to wipe, everybody in and on the truck, was pointing behind me. I am not understanding what in the hell they are pointing at, so I turn around with my pants around my knees, and toilet paper in my hand, there is a white pickup with two guys sitting inside looking right at me, and I don't mean far away, they were close up, and personal. My ass hanging out, my face red, I didn't know what to do but finish wiping. I put the used toilet paper in my pocket, I didn't want to throw it on the ground. I pulled my pants up, nodded a gesture of "hey how are you" and I got out of there. I climbed back up in the truck and buried my face in embarrassment, so on with the adventure. Well he happened to have an old car seat in the back, but you couldn't sit on it cause, it was drenched from the storm that came through about 12 hours earlier, thank god it didn't storm during the day and ruin everyone's weekend, but this seat was really wet like a sponge. He went up this short hill but the hill was very steep about 40 degrees and without telling anyone they all rolled back against the tailgate right where right where we landed on this soggy car seat and water flew everywhere.

It didn't make a difference if I just embarrassed myself taking a leak, because now I am totally drenched. I think I better get out of this truck before something real stupid or dangerous happens to me, no that can't happen. When we got to my sister's place, the truck caught my pants and ripped a big slit all the way down one side, GREAT. All this happened in several hours, all in all the weekend went okay except for the laugh at Sue day, a parade in my honor, that's one parade I don't care to do over. It's time to go home and I'd like to get there on one piece.

## THE END

# THE DARK WAIT

I was coming from where my parents lived and trying to get to back to where me and my son lived. We are at the bus station waiting which seemed like all day for the bus that would take us home, after which seemed like forever, finally came. Well wouldn't you know that my son has one of the worst cases of the runs I've ever seen. The bus is here and I'm covered in my son's aftermath, I had no diapers with me, cause my stay at my parents went over my stay limit so I ran short of supplies. I had to use paper towels out of the bathroom of the bus station, "great" now I had to get on this bus, I smell horrendous. I really couldn't clean him up at the bus station, so I put clean clothes over everything. There was a little bathroom on the bus, it was small but I could clean him up. All clean fresh clothes, I still had to use paper towels for a diaper, after that incident he went to underwear. The bus ride was about 2 hours, because it stopped at several places to drop off passengers or pick some up. It was about 1am the bus pulled into the home station, it was dark and very creepy. I still had to walk to the train station which was about a quarter of a mile. I was so afraid to walk in the dark with a small child on my hip, that's like wearing a sign that says come beat me up, take my child and use him against me, assault me and whatever they wanted. I felt better standing where the lights are and that made me more safe. I had to go to the train station by 1:30am and the clock was ticking. Well they always just say do it, so I started walking and the further I walked the smaller the light got and the dark set in. I got to the tracks and I knew they would take me to the station quicker but boy it was dark. The chill started going down my back, the hair on my neck standing up. I walked for about 20 minutes and made it to the station with no incidents, and do you know the fracking place was closed. Now we had to sit outside in the cold on a cold concrete slab. I figured the train would be there soon because it was going on 1:30am. Suddenly in the distance I could see three people coming up the tracks, now would be the time to panic. I got up and kind of standing in front of my son, which was still sitting on the ground. The people came up to me, I noticed they were young in their late teens, they are usually the worst kind of people to like terrorizing the town. I didn't say anything to them, and one of them said "you waiting for a train"? I kind of chuckled said yes and this person said, the reason I asked is because it's always late in the winter season. I asked how long would it be before it gets here. They said about a half an hour longer. They also said that if a put a sheet of newspaper on the concrete before I sit on it, it would keep me from getting piles. Now I'm no dummy, but I'm going to ask a stupid question "what are piles"? I didn't know and have never heard of it. It gives you hemorrhoids if you sit on concrete without having newspaper under you. I was surprised they knew that. They were also passing around something they had in a mason jar, and asked me if I wanted a drink. Sure, it was cold, I took a big gulp and about choked, it was moonshine, WOW it warmed me right up. They started to leave and asked me for another drink, I gladly took it and thanked them for the advice and the hot toddy, and they walked back up the tracks. The train finally came and we were on our way home. Sometimes it's not better to judge people before you know them, but these days you almost have to stay alert due to some other people that can't or won't do the right thing for themselves, their lost and will probably stay lost.

## THE END

# OLD MOTEL

There was this place and oh what a place it was, no it's not I hated it there, so did everyone else. I know my sisters hated it as well. School is number one on the list of things, besides the neighbors and the neighborhood. Every day it was a chore to go to school, because of the hassle we got everyday just going to school, getting fire crackers thrown under your dress at the bus stop, spit in your hair, rip threads out of your clothes as they sit behind you on the bus, making fun of your last name, I was very proud of my last name, but I didn't or maybe I did understand why they did the things they did to me. At a younger age I didn't really understand that, and as I got older my father would show us how to defend ourselves. It was so much harder, when there was more of them than there was of me or us. Later in life dad explained to us that people that do that to someone, especially when there was nothing wrong with you, it's pure jealousy. Maybe they are threatened that maybe you might have things that they don't, money, family, etc. Some people are like that, half of them are either clueless, jealous, or their parents didn't teach them any better, and I understand that now. School was a no no to us, we could teach each other better, and we did, because most of the time dad wanted to see our homework to prove that at least look like we went to school. One day we left for school and decided not to wait at the bus stop, which was a half a mile from our quarter of a mile driveway so we wouldn't have to put up with their crap for a half an hour before the bus comes. This day we changed our routine and decided to go to school but we wanted to try and walk, which is about another 3 to 5 miles extra, and we started our first time trip. We decided to walk along 301 and stay away from the back road so we don't run into dad or the mean kids. The trip showed us a new route, and bang there she was, an old broken down, motel. Now I know you think what could be the attraction to an old rickety building, the pool had about 3 feet of green sludge, get walking to school, don't even think about going in the motel, we needed to get to school, we all knew how this was going to go, that motel called to us, something to play in, new territory. The three of us went right into the motel, there were rooms, some had junk, paint peeling off the walls, garbage strewn around, old mattresses were in this one room piled up, there was about 60 of them. There was an old bar like room, there were old empty bottles, trashed up like the rest of the place. There were some shopping carts laying around, so we would act like we were shopping, sleeping overnight, pretending to have guests over, act like we were a family, maybe the family we needed, or maybe we were just brats, who knows. That day got away from us, we heard a car coming, thank god the drive to the motel started in the front of the building, so when we heard the car coming we ran in the room with all those mattresses in it, we squeezed in them like a cheese sandwich. This was a very large room, there was about 60 mattresses in it, so it was good camouflage for disappearing children. After we hid we heard someone come in and start yelling out to us, why I don't know.

How would anyone know that we were even in there. At first, we thought it might have been dad, and I know we weren't going to open our mouths, then whoever it was called out "children" I know you are in here come out, we stayed quiet as a church mouse. We knew it had to be the principle, we had heard him on several occasions when we skipped school, so we were well known to him. After several attempts of yelling out he left. We crawled out from in between the mattresses and went back to what we were doing. We jumped in the pool full of green crap, but we didn't care, maybe that's what's wrong with us now. After that we started walking to school but up the back roads. The motel wasn't a very good hide out when it sits along the highway. Kind of sounds like a horror story.

## THE END

# WRONG THOUGHTS

My husband and I lived in a small trailer. I was trying to remodel some of it, and decided to do the bathroom. I needed some help, or better yet someone to talk to. You tend to work better with someone to talk to while you work besides. My sister's husband, well we were more like brother and sister, even more like brothers and sisters that get along. He and I started on my bathroom where I was doing a lavender motif, so I got him to come over and after my husband went to work we started on it. If my husband would be there he would be asking stupid questions. We went and got the paper and paint and started. After we got everything almost done, I accidently broke the lightbulb in the bathroom. It wasn't a regular bulb, it was one of those long like tube lights, no problem I did have another one. Red said we should vacuum the floor, I said no, I'll just sweep it up, it will be fine. Well we went back to what we were doing and he, knelt down, on the carpet to finish the painting and he kind of yelled out he had something stuck in his knee and it was bleeding. We both ran out in the kitchen and I grabbed a large towel, because he had blood squirting out of his cut through his jeans. I'm in the kitchen, I have this bar like counter between my front door and my kitchen, so if you, knelt down, all you would see would be the top of your head. Well I quickly told him to drop his pants so I could get a better look at his wound. At this time, he was leaning against the sink facing me, I'm on my knees tending to his wound, and right at that minute, I thought what in the hell would happen if my husband or his wife would have walked in. This doesn't look very innocent but I didn't think of it at that time. I didn't take the glass out of his wound, I just wrapped it in a heavy white towel and took him to the ER. After the doctor looked at him and said that it was a good thing that we didn't pull out the glass, because it would have bled really bad, and may have been fatal, because of hitting a main vein. It's not always what you see, it's always what is going on, it would have been very hard to explain that one.

## THE END

# PURSE BE GONE

I had left home with my son and daughter to the Park, down by the water. This is where my father and my kids grandfather used to swim. He died and the age of 47 and close to 3 months after my daughter was born, so when she got to meet him, she wouldn't have remembered anyway. We were going swimming that day, beautiful sunny Saturday. I grabbed my purse, the diaper bag, spare clothes for the kids, extra milk for the baby, she was about 6 months old. This swimming place faces the river, just down the hill from the church were my dad was buried on the hill so he can look at the river for his place of final resting. We drove down and parked and walked down to the water it was about 50 yards from where you had to park your vehicle. I laid out a blanket so I could lay the baby down, it was a very good spot, slightly shaded, so she wouldn't get burned. I put sun block on my son, but he never cared about sun protection lotions, he would see water and go, but would only stay close to the shore, he was very close to mommy. When we walked down to the beach there where about 10 people, 2 or 3 older couples and 3 boys playing in the water, they aged in the range of 16 to 20. The baby's laying on the blanket and my son is playing in the water splashing around. Two of the boys were a good way out into the water playing around, they had to have been on their own, because I thought that one or two of the couples that were there were their parents, but as the day progressed the couples left one at a time, and the boys were parentless. My daughter fell asleep, and I wanted to go out and play with my son in the water, and I did for about 10 minutes. I saw that two of the boys were a way out in the water splashing around. I wanted to go swimming where it was a little deeper. Don't get me wrong, I love playing with my son but I needed a little swim before we headed home. When I went out where the two boys were playing around, when I turned to look up at the beach to make sure that the baby was still asleep, and to see what my son was doing the third boy was looking into my purse. I yelled "hey" and before I knew it the two boys that were on the water managed to get close to the bank and run out of the water to join their friend who now has my purse, and the baby's diaper bag, running up the hill out of sight. I ran as fast as I could, but water is the worst to run in. I yelled at them to stop, come back here, and they really had to have this planned. They seemed to wait until everyone was gone, so they could get away with it. Screaming at them had no effect at all, actually, the more I yelled the faster they ran. I got up to the blanket where my daughter was and they were out of sight. They took my purse, in it was the keys to the car, money, food stamps, driver's license, social security card, and a bunch of other important things. Then on top of that and for no good sake, I don't know why they would steal a diaper bag for, there was nothing in it that would even do anything for them, diapers, clothes, bottles, her medicine, shoes, the only 2 pair that she had. I know the bag wasn't of importance as to the contents, but the bag was a Jordash, that my aunt gave to me for the baby, I just wanted to point that out. Now I have no food for the kids, I had snacks in the bag, no keys to the car, so I can't get the kids home. It was getting dark, no phone to call the police, what in God's creation are we going to do? There is no one in sight, and you can't see us from the road, and the road being a back road off a back road, I mean in the woods. I had to do something I really didn't want to do, but I had no choice, but to bust the steering wheel column to unlock the mechanism that locks the steering wheel when the switch is turned in the off position. You have to bust the column around the steering wheel to turn the key slot, thank god I knew how to do that, it's from being around dad growing up and experience from breaking down along the highway, and just knowing how to do it really helped. When I did that, I went straight to the police department and reported the crime. I was so pissed that they would take a diaper bag from a baby, what am I carrying golden pampers, silver dollar rubber pants, or maybe diamond cut baby bottles, come on really. After about 7 days the police department called and said that they found the diaper bag, they had rooted through it and tossed it in the woods, not leave it in the road so I could have my kid's stuff. A day or so later they called and said they found my purse floating in a creek behind some apartment complex. All the stuff was ruined, the stamps were destroyed, I had to report that to be replaced. I had to replace, all of my cards, they took the money, about $15, I hope it was worth it. After about 2 more weeks go by, I got court papers in the mail with 3 different court cases against these 3 boys verses me. I don't know how they found them, but did. I went to court, it was real hard to face them, because the last time I saw them was the back of their heads as they were running up the hill with my property, right after they conned me away from my stuff and got my guard down and took off. Pure parenting gone wrong, another child of bad parenting so I thought. The day of court the boys had fathers with them. I didn't see any mothers there, which I thought was odd, but it made sense to me. I figure these three boys got into trouble because of a broken home, and because of that of that the world owes them something. One of the fathers didn't seem to be mad, now the other two boys their fathers were a bit, more irate. One father slapped the boy right in the back of the head and I mean full slap right after the judge sentenced them to community service and restitution of $40 each payable to me. After he slapped the boy he, asked "what is wrong with you"? and headed him out of the courthouse. The third boy, his father made him come over to me and my two kids and apologize to me for stealing my stuff. I said to the boy, I know your reasoning for stealing my purse which was wrong, but why would you steal a diaper bag from a child. The hope of finding something worth something, instead they choose the life of crime. I don't know if that was their plan all along, yes let's rob a defenseless woman and her two children. I hope that they learned something from this experience, but from my point, I doubt that they changed. I'm sure in the far future they will be looking from the other side of the bars. It's things like this that really make it hard to trust people ever.

THE END

# ORANGE BICYCLE

One weekend my husband, son and myself decided to go to my brothers who lived 20 miles from me. I usually would go to my brothers after work, stop at the store, get a pack of cigarettes, and a roll of toilet paper for them, they always needed cigarettes. The toilet paper was because we used theirs up so I brought my own. I left it there, weather we used it or not, it was the point. My husband wanted to come too, he had a very bright bike painted neon orange, you could see that thing from a mile or so. He wanted to take it so he could ride around town when we go to my brother's house because he lived close to town and it was easier to ride his bike there. On that Sunday, it was time to go back home, about 20 miles. My husband goes outside to put the bike in the trunk of the car, before we leave. I was talking to my brother and his wife for a while, and about 20 minutes goes by, and I hadn't heard from him come back in the house to say all loaded up lets go. After a while we all went outside to look, we thought that he was on his bike riding up and down the street. No husband and no bright orange bicycle, nowhere in sight. I called several people and no one had seen him anywhere. I get in the car, get the boy strapped in, and look around town to see if I can find him. Well after looking for about an hour, I drive back to my brothers and asked if he came back, no one had seen him. I told them I'm going home and put my son to bed, maybe he decided to petal home for 20 miles, I don't know but if I see him I'm going to strangle him for worrying me like this. I drove real slow going home to my house, no husband, he never made it home. Well the next thing I know the phone rings, it's him, he says he's at the lake at the store, it's about half of the way home. I told him to stay there I was coming and not to move an inch. I was already hot, and it was winter time so it was cold. I had to put some oil in my car, but the stuff was pouring in so slow, because the oil was so cold it was as thick as molasses, I had to put it in the car before I went to go get him. I did that then went to go get this man and scream at him for a minute. Taking off without telling anybody. I get to the store and he's not there, where in the hell is he. I go into the store and ask if anyone has seen a large man on a neon orange bicycle. No one has seen him, so now my worry and anger have turned into rage. I am going to skin that man alive if I find out he is okay, then I will kill him. I left the store wondering where in the hell could he have gone to. Again,I head home wondering why he would call me and then take off. When I got home he was there, I asked him why in the hell did you take off from the store, you knew I was coming to get you, and I told you not to go anywhere. He said the first time when I left your brothers place, and you were looking for me I was in a ditch because I lost control of the bicycle, and saw me go right by him, but it was dusk outside, it was really hard to see at night, but why did you leave the store, do you think it's funny scaring people like that? My brother, and his family and some of the other kids were looking for you. I wanted to bike home he says, it was like talking to a wall. I think the alcohol contributed to his behavior, but he has always been good at pissing people off.

## THE END

# COLD RIDE

I met this guy named in high school, he was cute enough. After knowing him a while, I realized that he was in my math class, he sat all the way in the back of the classroom. I guess it was so the teacher won't call on him. I had to sit in the front because I couldn't see the board, it could have been screwed to my nose and I still wouldn't have been able to see it. It's like I always say, I could hear a mosquito peeing a mile away, but I couldn't see him jacking off on my nose, which means that I am as bling as a bat. That day I found out the he sat in the back of the room, the teacher called out to him and called him. I laughed along with everyone else on the class, because he was called on anyway. When I looked around to the voice that answered the teacher, it was him. I met his mother, she was a sweet lady, and she worked at the in town. Somehow, he and I stated dating, on the weekends we would use his moms car and we would go Dutch, and get a pizza, go to the drive in. Nobody goes to the drive-in to watch the movie, they go to neck and do whatever you can't do at home. I necked but that was it, I was a good girl, not a princess, but I had scruples, who knew if he was the one for me. After a while I would go out to his mother's and do some household stuff for her like dishes, make beds, vacuum, dust, or whatever she needed, and on the plus side I got to eye her son while I did my work. The woman really impressed me, besides working full time she was involved with the church, so she was a very interesting woman, I couldn't remember what happened to his father, I never saw him or met him. Whenever she would need me, she would send her son on his motor bike to come get me for a couple of hours. It was usually at the end of the week so I would have money for the moves and pizza and he would do the same, earn extra money for the same reason. One day he came to get me, usually I could her him coming because the road to his moms ends up just past the tracks in front of my house. There was my house, the street, a big hill, the river, the railroad tracks, then the road to his moms, only there was a train depot at the end of our street, so I had like 5 minutes to put my shoes on, put my hair up so it wouldn't slap me in the face, when I heard him coming, and that was all that was needed because it was a beautiful day. It seemed as though he was hitting every pothole he could find, thank God I had a helmet on. The air was starting to get cold, because I didn't put on a sweater. We weren't going that far so I didn't think I needed all that. Well for some reason he was going to his house by a road that was not familiar to me at all. I tapped him on the shoulder and asked him where in the hell is he going, he mumbles something and I shrugged it off, but I was getting cold. Finally, we got to his house, not noticing I went in the house, I was really cold. He started a fire in the fire place, which he never did. I asked where his mother was, because I didn't see her or her car in the driveway. He wouldn't answer me as to where she was. I started to clean her kitchen as I always did, and at this time, he and I were taking time apart, because he blamed me for his grades being really bad. I know he spent too much time in the boys room smoking cigarettes, but I know it wasn't me. I still had a job to do, so I ignored what he was doing. I continued to start in the kitchen and he came up behind me, like we were still together, you know hugging me from behind. I jerked away from him and asked him what he was doing, he was acting very strange. He started chasing me around the kitchen table, it's like he was shot with something. The next thing I know is he's got the edge of my shirt and managed to get it off of me, so now I am exposed in a bra, but still exposed. I'm hollering at him asking where his mother was. He finally said to me that she was out of town. "Out of town" so why am I here, he let the cat out of the bag. It was his plan to act like I was going to clean for his mother, him picking me up routine, that the first time a man went that far to be with me. I thought it was kind of cute, and well you know what happened next, no need to go into detail, some of you would live that. The whole scenario of the failing grades I thought was coming from his mother to cut his extra activities down, so he can concentrate more in school, but it was him. His mother said that she loved having me around. I was mad at him for that, but he broke up with me for that reason, but the thing is his grades got worse, couldn't really understand that, so I wasn't the problem. I even could have helped him or help each other. He was one of the boys that my dad liked, and mom she liked a little too much … … … … The incident at the house must have been a romp to him, but I took it very serious, he even gave me a $150 watch that he and his mom picked out, and this very large winter coat. I felt that everything was fine for about a week, then I saw them. He was with his lips wrapped around some bimbo, so that's why his grades were going to the dogs, because he's leading a double life. He didn't see me at the time, but on this day we met at the lockers and I gave him back his coat and his watch and kissed him bye, put my chin up and walked off. My heart was breaking because I really loved him. I went around the corner to see what he was going to do after I walked off, he slammed the lockers with his fist, and kicked it really hard, about 4 times, but I wondered why, if he was into this other girl why would it make him mad for me to end things. I'm assuming he figured he could keep this up and no one would know, well except me, so long, it was a nice ride.

## THE END

# THE FACE

My two sisters myself were in this foster home. The woman of the place was old as dirt, and she's going to take care of three teenagers, OK. The woman that drove us there would always be drunk as a skunk and that would be scary. While we were living with her, she had us do so many chores, chop, spear, and hang tobacco, and then do the gardening, and by that time, the day would be over, and time to go to bed. When it was time for bed and once you were in bed you had to stay in bed. She didn't like you roaming around at night, but I got so thirsty I came downstairs to get a drink of water without anyone noticing, which wasn't easy, because the stairs creaked. Well I got up, tiptoed down the stairs, got a small glass, turned the spigot on, and filled the glass. I put the glass to my lips, as I tilted my head back to drink there was a face that came right towards the window, all I could see was the eyes and teeth, and the rest was red. I dropped the glass and ran like hell back to bed and I never did that again, next time I'll just dry up.

\*\*\*

# WEIRDO'S

My husband and I were living, close to a big city, I mean we were living right on the city/county line, there are several junk yards around. A friend of mine needed some tires for her car bad since she had no clue how to do that without buying them new, I told her we could go to the junk yard called crazy rays. It was a very large place, very easy to get lost in. You go in and get your own stuff off, and then you walk to the window and pay for your items. I carried a tire iron so when and if we find any tires, I would have to take them off myself, not an easy task. I used my sister's car to go to the junk yard. My girlfriend went with me so she could watch my son while I do her dirty work. It wasn't too bad, except this day it was really muddy so that made it real fun. I walked through the gate, which it cost $1 to get in, even if you don't find what you are looking for. I went in and walked around for what seemed like hours, so I could start at the back of the property and work my way forwards, but when I got back there, there was this real creepy feeling and a very bad odor, like when a body starts to decompose. I don't know exactly how a body smells, but I do know what an animal smells like when it rots and I'm assuming they smell the same when it rots, it was bad. I immediately turned around and started on my way back, that was far enough. I started looking for her tire and 90% of the cars didn't have wheels, and the ones that did were flat or didn't fit, wrong size. I quit looking, there wasn't anything here for her car. All a sudden I noticed this guy following me, just to be sure, I keep looking over my shoulder, I continued like I was doing before I noticed him. I would turn up on one side of a junk car, walk a way, and he would do the same, then just to be sure he was following me, I would look up and he would look away, like he was doing no wrong, bending down looking at something. I ducked behind this black Cadillac, it's hood was up, and looked between the opening of the hood of the car, it made a great cover. When I did pop my head up to see if he was still there, he was looking around as if he had lost something, he was looking for me, he was looking in my general direction because that is where he saw me last. I kept down, then began to stalk him to see where he came from. When I did meet up with about 4 or 5 of his either family or friends, I don't know who, but I got the hell out of there. I told her to buy tires because there wasn't any there. Sometimes it pays to buy new tires.

***

# FREE BACON

When I was a child, not that I was a good child, every time mom would go to the store we would tag along. Mom didn't like it, and on this day mom was going grocery shopping, and that meant a couple of hours of non-stop shopping "shoplifting let me correct that. We had this station wagon with a wooden box in it for small pieces of wood for the stove, but it was empty at the time, or was it? Mom says watch the kids I'm going to the store, dad would wave his hand as if he heard her. Mom leaves the house, gets to the store and we pop up from behind the seat and she would be mad, but what can she do at this point. It was my three sisters and my brother, the youngest sister that went with us was always good for acting like a baby when I would nab the stroller. I would put her in one, take the price tag off and act like I was her mom or babysitter and roll right out of the store. When we let mom know we were there she was always mad, but she's always mad it never made a difference what we were doing, so why not get under her skin at the grocery store. We went in the store with mom, and mom being such a good role model hands me a half pound of bacon. I slipped it under my shirt in the back of my pants. After that I decided to go to the department store that was next door to see if I could find something over there. I really needed a gift for a boy at school. It was his birthday and I really wanted to get him something and maybe something for myself, look at me go ... I'm thinking about others, and myself all due to a five finger discount. Well I found the perfect thing for this boy, some match box cars, and I spotted this pair of pants and had to have them, the clothes I have are holey. I know mom and dad weren't rich, but it would help at school so the kids wouldn't beat me up. I took them off the hanger, rolled them up and stuffed them and the cars in my purse like thing I had with me. I was heading out to the car to get rid of that loot I had in my bag, I could see the doors, there they are. Stop a guy stands in front of me and asked me where I was going. I told him I was looking for my mother, he reaches in his pocket and takes out a badge, oh great a cop, lovely just what I need. Well the store police only saw what I was doing, the rest of my family was still roaming the store robbing it blind. The store police placed me against the wall, right in the clothing area where I took the pants, and searched me but didn't find anything on my body, but plenty in my bag. He took me to this room in the back of the store, I was scared, not of the store police, and not even mom, I was worried about dad finding out about what I or we did. I can't speak for the other kids, but I'm in a pickle. Well they say we need to call your folks, what's your house number. I told them that we don't have a phone, but we did, but I did tell them that my mom was in the store next door shopping. one cop comes back with her and she looks at me, like you bad girl, but she's probably just as guilty. The officer asked my mom, "do you know what your daughter had done"? No, what? She had stolen match box cars and a pair of pants, the store police asked me where was the top that went with the pants. I said, "I don't know cause if there was a top that went with them I would have stolen that too". They asked who the cars were for and I told them that they were for a kid at school and that it was his birthday. Again, a different cop searched me, thought I was lying about the shirt. He finally let me go into my mom's custody, and we got out to the car, the wooden box was full of stuff, like clocks, shoes, clothes, toys, you name it. I started laughing just before we got to the car. Mom said what on god's green earth could you have to laugh about. Well yes, I do, because I reached into my pants in the back where I had that half pound of bacon and it was still there. Those store police searched me twice and didn't find it, even mom had to laugh.

## THE END

# CLEAN UP CREW

My husband and I moved into my sister's house, well apartment so I can babysit her 4 kids. I think I was there a couple of months and those kids had crap everywhere. All the stuff I had in the closet they broke, the wall was covered in crayon, she would let them write all over the wall. Luckily it was only the hallway walls, it looked like a coloring book gone bad. I had a little idea to get them to clean their mess. I got out a little pot, a rag and a scrub pad and sat close to the wall, and started to clean small patches of crayon, and I would giggle a little and look around to see if anyone was looking, you know like a kid caught in a cookie jar. So, the more I did this the more interested the younger kids became, and when they would get close to see what I was doing, the more I would try to hide it, you know how nosy kids are. I kept that up until I had every one of the kids scrubbing the crayon off the wall, I sat back and watched. I set up a plan, I got each one of the kids a paper sack and said whoever collets the most trash would get the prize, or maybe 50 cents or to go to the park. It worked the house was crayon and trash free. Sometimes you had to stoop lower to be at their level.

\*\*\*

# BOBCAT

Where we lived was real creepy at night. Every time us kids would go to bed there would be this crawling noise scratching at the ceiling from the attic you could hear it. It was very heavy at one point, this thing had somehow managed to get its paw through one of the ceiling tiles or board, I'm not sure. What I am sure of it was a big paw, the size of a small plate, white fur, long nails, and this thing had a real bad growl, it scared us not knowing what this thing was. My parents room was at one end of the house and the kitchen was at the other, but when you stood in my parent's door facing out you were facing the kitchen. One day in the middle of the afternoon we were sitting on our beds in the room between my parent's room and the kitchen, playing cards or something like that. We heard a crash and right in the kitchen window was this humongous cat, if it was a house cat it had to have had one hell of a mother. This thing was big, it's head was the size of a large bowling ball, it had a collar on it, so it had to have belonged to someone, but who the jolly green giant, this thing was the size of a small bear or a tiger. It jumped onto the window sill and we all froze, mom told us one by one slowly to get off the bed and come into the

141

bedroom where she was, in case this thing wants to eat a small child. It was surprising she didn't try to feed us to the cat. We all got in the room and mom got the 22 semi, auto and it was always loaded cause dad had loaded guns all over the house. Mom aimed at that thing and shot it, it did nothing, then she shot it again, it looked in her direction as to attack whoever it was that was shooting it, mom shot again, finally after 4 or 5 shots it fell out the window. We went out there a couple of days later and it was big, so we took it away from the house because it was drawing flies and starting to stink. No more kitty.

THE END

# GREEN PAINT

This place that we lived as children was very back in the woods, and the neighborhood was not the best. One day me and my sisters and brother went for a walk. Doesn't seem the trouble is always in the pack of us 3 or 4 family members, but as you read on you will understand we band together thick as thieves. Just before you get to our bus stop, the one we never go to anymore, there was this abandoned old house. The house itself was okay, but it looked like it had been in a fire and then about 10 years of abuse, weather, wind, and all the windows were gone. The upstairs was a little iffy as the stairs going up were broken, not too sure about them, so we used the edge along the wall to get upstairs. We got up the stairs and there were about 10 cans of old paint still closed, and my brother found a bottle of vodka. We went outside to see the rest of the house, because this house was very large. Out back it was all over grown with vines and bushes that had the things on it that would stick all over you. Instead of fighting with them, we could collect them and build things with them like purses, ties, hats, not really good for hats because I tried that once and it took me 3 times longer to get them out of my hair, then off of my clothes. Well we did that for a couple of hours, and that got boring so we went in the house. DJ decided to drink the vodka at the age of 4, I figured he would of tasted it then spit it out and that would be the end of it, but no, he continued to sip it throughout the day. Upstairs was the paint, maybe we could paint the house, that was our intention, but we couldn't find any paint brushes, what to do. Shoot we dipped our hands right in the paint which was a neon green paint. Why I don't know but it was a lot of paint, they were about all half full so we each had our own bucket. I don't know what caused it but we were throwing paint at each other, we started smearing it everywhere, in our hair, face, clothes, not realizing this is house paint, and it's not going to come out of our hair, or off our skin. At about 4pm at least we thought it was, most of the time we are shoved outside all day with nothing to eat or drink unless we can convince mom to feed us. Oh yeah, she cracks open a window about 6 inches and shoves a loaf of bread and a gallon of water under a 6 inch, crack, that's was the 5 of us had to eat all day, and wonder why we get into trouble, the only direction from my mother was "get away from the window". Any way we got home and dad was already home from work and was firing mad because he had no idea where we were, maybe mom told dad she didn't know where we were. We stood there and knew we were in very hot water, and I mean that literally. He stuck us in a hot bath, and got a bucket of turpentine paint remover and scrubbed us down, that stuff burned our skin, and the paint wouldn't come out of our hair, so dad shaved us bald, as bald as a bowling ball. Do you know how embarrassing it is not to have any, hair. Thank god it was not during the school season, because the kids were very nasty to us as it was, we didn't need to add a comedy show of the bowling balls.

THE END

# THE FISH TANK

I was coming from one foster home to another, and when I got there I noticed that they had a son, but oddly enough they were preppy, neat freaks. We had to say grace before dinner and everything had to be ahead of schedule. You could not be a normal kid in the house. The kid and I got along while the parents were around, but when we played together after they would leave the room the kid was always snatching things out of my hand and everything was his. One day his parents went out to the store and left me there to babysit him. They had this living room that we were not supposed to be in where they had this humongous fish tank, plastic on the couches, and expensive rugs. He went into the kitchen and got a hand held mixer and was chasing me and winding my hair up in the mixer. To be able to get away from him I ran into the off-limits room and he followed me. He came at me with the mixer again and I pushed him and he threw the mixer across the room and it hit the fish tank. Well guess what, the damn fish tank exploded, and now there is a tsunami in the living room with fish flopping all over the floor and water steadily flowing. I got a pot to try and collect the fish off the expensive rugs, and you know they walked in the door. The stupid kid blamed me for the whole thing saying that I threw the mixer at him. They made a phone call to the social worker and they came to take me to another foster home that evening and they took me to another home. I guess even when people take you in as part of their family they should treat you like part of the family.

THE END

# NO STARTER NO CAR

I was married for only about a year, to this guy, not the brightest crayon in the box. We came up to the mountains to visit my mother, why she never gave a good dam whether I showed up or not. I came up with my husband and my two children. When we headed back to where we live. We were in a lime green car and a few friends thought it would be a good idea to put a bigger motor in it. The motor was so much bigger then the engine compartment would hold. Now we had to tie the hood down to keep it from flying up. On the way, out of town doing about 60 miles per hour and the hood caught wind and flew up to where I couldn't see almost wrecked the car, we pulled the car over and fixed the hood. We continued our journey. We got just a few miles and we stopped at this gas station and when we were trying to leave the car would not start. The starter went out in the car. We went back into the little gas station to call someone to bring us a starter. We wait a while and the guy comes with the starter. While the rest of us wait inside the gas station, He would put the starter on the car and we are out of here. I figure a simple job, A few minutes go by and my husband comes in the gas station and hands me my, drivers, license, and $75.00. I stared at him dumbfounded. What? What is this? He said that he couldn't get the starter to work so he sold my car while I was in the gas station. Well let's see if I can get this right. You get the starter and you say it didn't work and since it didn't work, so you sold my car. He sold my car to this stranger with all, of our stuff in it, my tags, everything. Did you check the starter, real, good? Because they tend to stick when they have been sitting a while. He said that he didn't. At this time, I was so mad, I went outside and took the starter and tapped it on the ground a couple of times, hooked it up to the battery the guy at the gas station had, and the starter Bendix popped out, which means that the starter works after all. You gave a perfect stranger has my tags title and you are trusting him to mail them to us. I was so mad at that point that I told him that he better, find us a ride home or you are history. After a while of waiting for a ride, here comes our ride and it was the same crap we were, in except it was a hatch back. I said that we better get home in time for him to go to work. The guy did send me my tags. But that situation should have not happened at all, what makes me mad is that he should have known that and he didn't. A good waste of air.

## THE END

Printed in the United States
By Bookmasters